MONOGRAPHS ON ARTISTS

MONOGRAPHS ON ARTISTS

EDITED, AND WRITTEN JOINTLY WITH OTHER AUTHORS,

BY

H. KNACKFUSS

II.

HOLBEIN

BIELEFELD AND LEIPZIG

VELHAGEN & KLASING

1899

HOLBEIN

BY

H. KNACKFUSS

TRANSLATED BY

CAMPBELL DODGSON

WITH 151 ILLUSTRATIONS FROM PICTURES AND DRAWINGS

BIELEFELD AND LEIPZIG

VELHAGEN & KLASING

1899

Printed by Fischer & Wittig, Leipzig.

(Frontispiece) PORTRAIT OF A MAN UNKNOWN. Body-colour.
In the Royal Print-Cabinet, Berlin.

The boys "Prosy" and "Hanns Holbain", drawn by their father, Hans Holbein the Elder; at the top the date 1511, near to Hans a note of his age (14); a similar note by the side of the elder brother is no longer legible. Silver-point drawing in the Royal Print Cabinet, Berlin.

HANS HOLBEIN.

IT is usual to name Dürer and Holbein together in speaking of German art of the Renaissance at its zenith. But it would be wrong to attempt an immediate comparison of the two great masters with one another. The difference in age between them, more than a quarter of a century, is enough in itself to preclude this. It is a difference which counts for very much at a time so full of vigorous, stirring life as was the century of transition from the Middle Ages to modern times. Then, too, the greatness of the two masters lies in essentially different spheres. Dürer's imagination had a creative force to which no other German painter has ever attained. In the gift of invention, in intelligence, in feeling and also in culture, Dürer stands far above Holbein. But the latter, unlike Dürer, was a true painter. Colour, to him, is not a mere cloak to the shapes which he calls into being; it is something essential, of the inmost being of his art; it is a means of expressing his artistic perception. Dürer issued from a school which was still half under the sway of the Gothic style, and it was by his genius that he discovered the paths which the new art was to follow. Holbein, on the other hand, was in no way connected with the art of the

Middle Ages. He was trained by his father, who had fully kept pace with the Renaissance, and this had reached its maturity by the time that the boy, born in the year 1497, was capable of receiving instruction in art and turning it to account. So we have no need to school ourselves in the language of form which Holbein uses; it is immediately intelligible to us.

A talent for art is seldom hereditary. Hans Holbein, however, possessed the germ of the gift which made him great as his inheritance by birth from his father. The latter also had the Christian name of Hans, and in the history of art the suffix "the Elder" or "the Younger" is added, to distinguish the two painters of the same name. When "Hans Holbein" simply is mentioned, the younger of the two is always meant. But Hans Holbein the Elder also fills a very honourable place in the history of German art. Born at Augsburg — in what year is not known — as the son of a master -tanner, who had immigrated from the neighbouring community of Schöne-feld, he devoted himself to painting, as did one of his brothers, by name Siegmund. We have records of his works from the year 1492 or 1493 onwards. We observe in them the influence of the works of that great and charming master, Martin Schongauer, whose engravings had a world-wide circulation, while it is possible that the Augsburg painter may have worked as pupil in his much-frequented studio at Colmar. There is, further, to be recognised in them a decided acceptance of that tendency which had been started by the works of the brothers van Eyck, with their loving reproduction of nature and their deep poetry of colour. The sense for an exact rendering of what was actually before him declared itself in the elder Holbein most decidedly in his liking and capacity for grasping the human countenance in all its variety and with the exact peculiarities which each face displays. His sacred pictures are full of persons who are visibly taken from actual life, portraits of men who lived as contemporaries of the painter. Of especial interest for us is a group of persons who are introduced as spectators of the baptism of St. Paul in a picture now in the Augsburg Gallery: the master stands there himself with two boys aged about seven and five respectively, his sons Ambrosius and Hans; the former, the elder of the two, characterized as a schoolboy by the writing-apparatus attached to his girdle, seems to be of a lively temperament; the little Hans gives us the impression of a calm, quietly observant child; large, attentive eyes look out from his round face. Orders for portraits were probably hardly yet known at that time at Augsburg. The elder Holbein, accordingly, satisfied his liking for portraiture by drawing the persons of his acquaintance, high and low, in his sketch-book. A quantity of such leaves from a sketch-book are preserved, the greatest number of them being in the Print-room of the Berlin Museum. They are masterpieces of the art of portraiture, speaking likenesses of persons, clearly characterized and full of life, sketched by a light and sure hand, with fine execution aud a true painter's feeling, in silver-point, helped out now and then by red chalk or a touch of white, Among these drawings we find the heads of the two boys once more.

Fig. 1. The Virgin and Child. Oil-painting of the year 1514.
In the Basle Museum.

Fig. 2. THE VIRGIN MARY. Oil-painting in the Basle Museum.
(After an original photograph by Braun, Clément & Co., Dornach (Alsace)
and Paris.)

A leaf in the Berlin Print-room, marked with the date 1511, shows them facing one another, with their names written near them. The curly "Prosy" appears here already as a youth; "Hanns", whose age is indicated as fourteen, shows, under hair combed simply down, a round, childish face, in which the likeness to the earlier portrait is still very great.

The elder Holbein became in the first decade of the sixteenth century an enthusiastic adherent of the new tendency in art, which was introduced from Italy. There are extant pictures by him dating from the year 1508 onwards which completely belong to the style of the Renaissance, not only in the external sense that in the architecture and decorative frames of the pictures antique forms have taken the place of the Gothic, but also in this essential respect, that the figures have acquired a greater roundness and softness of form, the drapery has a freer, larger cast, and all the lines a more animated impulse. His altar-piece in the Pinakothek at Munich, the "Altar of St. Sebastian", is one of the gems of German painting in the Renaissance style.

In spite of the esteem which the elder Holbein enjoyed as a painter, he fared badly in his old age. He left Augsburg in the year 1517, on account of financial difficulties, and died in 1524 at Isenheim in Alsace.

His sons, both of whom he had educated to succeed him in the practice of his art, left their native town even earlier and betook themselves to Basle, where there is evidence for the activity of Hans Holbein from 1515 and for that of Ambrosius from 1516 onwards.

Ambrosius Holbein was gifted with a modest talent. Only a few pictures by him are extant; among these two portraits of boys, in the Basle Museum, hold the first place. There are, further, a few portrait-drawings by him, preserved in the same collection and in the Albertina at Vienna. To these must be added a number of designs reproduced as woodcuts, for the most part title-pages richly ornamented and decked out with allegorical subjects. Ambrosius Holbein must have died early. His reception into the Basle Guild of painters is recorded in a document of the year 1517. After 1519, however, there is no work or document which gives any further evidence of his existence.

Hans Holbein drew attention to himself at the very outset of his residence at Basle by striking and important works.

The Basle Museum possesses the earliest known work by the hand of Hans Holbein the Younger, a small picture of the Virgin,

Fig. 3. ST. JOHN THE EVANGELIST. Oil-painting in the Basle Museum. (After an original photograph by Braun, Clément & Co., Dornach (Alsace) and Paris.)

signed with the date 1514 (Fig. 1). This little picture was discovered in a village in the neighbourhood of Constance, and the supposition seems well founded, that the young painter produced it during his emigration from Augsburg to Basle. It is a childish, but attractive work. The Virgin Mary is represented sitting, half-length, holding the infant Christ on her lap. She wears a white dress and black cloak. The dress, which falls into delicate folds, is adorned with gold embroidery; face and hands and the little body of the child are so light in tone that their colour approximates to white. The whole group, so quiet in tone, stands out against a dark-red background, which, however, does not immediately touch the white of the dress and the colourless flesh, but is separated from them by the gold of the crown on the Virgin's head and of the hair which falls over her shoulders. Round the little picture is a painted frame resembling an erection of white stone, on which little angels move about, standing in relief against black panels of ornament in the architectural structure; these carry the instruments of Christ's Passion, musical instruments and small tablets for inscriptions. From the cross-piece at the top of this frame a green laurel-wreath hangs down on the dark red background, which is further enlivened by two coats-of-arms. The motives of the frame belong entirely to the Renaissance style. The delightful harmony produced by the few tints already evinces a great delicacy of feeling for colour.

Among the works of Holbein's hand collected by his friend Bonifacius Amerbach, which form the foundation of the collection in the Basle Museum,

Fig. 4. THE LAST SUPPER. Oil-painting on canvas.
In the Basle Museum.

several pictures are expressly mentioned in the original catalogue as the earliest works of the master. These must, accordingly, belong to the first year of his residence at Basle, 1515. They consist of two heads of saints and a number of pictures of the Passion of Christ. The two saints, a virgin with crown and loose hair (Fig. 2) and a beardless young man with curly hair (Fig. 3), represent perhaps Mary and John the Evangelist. They have golden nimbi and light-blue backgrounds. The tones here, too, are well harmonized. But in form and expression the carefully painted heads do not yet betray much of the high gift of their author.

The pictures of the Passion are calculated in a higher degree to rivet our attention. The pieces derived from the Amerbach collection, to which the old list has attached the notice quoted above in regard to the date of their origin, represent the Last Supper and the Scourging of Christ. In addition to these, three others which have found their way to the Basle Museum by later acquisitions, obtriously form part of the same series, which was,

no doubt, originally larger. These are: the prayer on the Mount of
Olives, Christ taken captive and Pilate washing his hands. The pictures
are painted, not on panels, but on canvas. Since at that date in Germany
this was still quite unusual in the case of pictures which were considered
valuable, the hypothesis has been reasonably put forward that they were
painted for some temporary purpose, perhaps for the decoration of a church
during Holy Week. This would also explain the hard and hasty style of
execution of these pictures. It has also been thought necessary to suppose,

Fig. 5. THE SCOURGING. Oil-painting on canvas.
In the Basle Museum.

since these pictures do not at first sight give one the impression of works by
Holbein, that he carried them out in the studio of an older painter in the
capacity of his assistant. According to this assumption, the composition of the

Fig. 6. PORTRAIT OF A MAN UNKNOWN. Oil-painting of 1515.
In the Grand-Ducal Museum, Darmstadt.

pictures would probably not be his own, but would proceed from the master
of the studio. But the compositions are more important than one would
expect from one of the older Basle painters of that time, and in two things
Holbein's special gifts find clear expression: in the artistic value of the

scheme of colour, and in the vivacity and naturalness of the countenances; the expression of the faces is everywhere extraordinarily eloquent, and even if it borders on exaggeration here and there, that is easy to explain in the case of pictures in which the hard style of execution admitted no refinements.

In the representation of the Last Supper (Fig. 4) the scene is laid in a room of fanciful and ornamental Renaissance architecture — an architecture which is quite Holbein's own, — through openings in which the dark-blue sky appears. The supper is laid on two tables which are placed at right angles to one another. Christ sits at the angle so as to be seen from the side and passes the bread across the table to Judas, who is dressed in yellow. The effect of colour in the whole is very rich. In a kind of colonnade, which is seen in the background, the washing of Peter's feet is introduced as a secondary subject.

Fig. 7.   Concluding vignette to Erasmus' "PRAISE OF FOLLY".   (Folly descends from the lecturer's chair).
Pen-drawing in the copy which belonged to Erasmus, in the Basle Museum.

The prayer on the Mount of Olives is the subject of a dark nocturne. Christ throws up his arms with a violent movement, according to the precedent of Dürer's engraved Passion, which had appeared a few years before. The angel, boldly foreshortened, comes head-foremost down from heaven; he wears a light-red Renaissance costume. The raiment of the Saviour and that of St. Peter, who lies asleep in the foreground, harmonize in their black tones with the general night-effect. On the horizon there is a glimmer of the red light of dawn in the clouds. A bright light proceeds from the torches of the men who are stepping through the gate of the garden in the background. If this picture produces on the whole a less pleasing effect than the rest, the treatment of the next event which follows, the betrayal of Christ, is truly great and impressive. A turbulent movement runs through the picture, in which, as usual, the three moments of the kiss of Judas, the arrest of the master whom he has betrayed and Peter's stroke with the sword are combined. The peculiar force of the impression which the colouring makes rests principally on the relation of the yellow coat of Judas to the grey steel of the armour and weapons of the henchmen; the torchlight is not employed for effects of artificial illumination.

Fig. 8. Ornamental border with the story of Tantalus. In the text, ornamental initial with Samson and Delilah. Woodcut.

In the picture of Pilate the left half of the painting is wrought out in a colour-scheme of great beauty. The Roman governor, in a coat of dark olive-green trimmed with ermine, is enthroned in a recess of variegated marble and washes his hands in a golden dish which a servant in dark clothes holds before him, whilst another servant, clad in a light yellow coat with black velvet, pours the water from a golden ewer. To the right of this group we see the Saviour, who is dragged out at the door by a band of men-at-arms; here the dark-blue of Christ's coat is the colour which tells most.

The Scourging is painted in a truly ruthless way and with a great impression of violence (Fig. 5). Christ, stripped of his clothes (remarkable

Fig. 9. Printer's mark of Johannes Froben. Woodcut.

knowledge being displayed in the drawing of the body), is bound with a cord passed round him to a white pillar; his hands are drawn up over his head with another cord; under the influence of violent pain he presses one leg convulsively across the other. The pale form of the Saviour and the savage gaolers in their clothes of bright colours stand out against a grey stone wall in the shade; in the wall we see the opening of a door, through which Pilate witnesses the gruesome spectacle.

In the versatility of his mind, Holbein, who had here depicted the bitterest suffering with such penetrating insight, was able to show an equal power of expression in the region of cheerful humour. The first proof of this is given by a work preserved in the Town Library at Zürich, which must have been produced in the first half of the year 1515, since Hans Ber, who gave the order for it, marched out in the summer of this year as standard-bearer with the troops from Basle, and did not return from the bloody fight of two days at Marignano. This is a wooden table painted with illustrations of popular jests. The principal subjects are a sleeping pedlar, whose wares are plundered by monkeys, and the "Nobody", who is accused of everything that goes wrong anywhere and is incapable of defending himself. Round these principal subjects is a frame in which all kinds of pastimes are represented; tournaments, hunting, fishing, bathing, feasting and girl-catching. Besides these, various little things, a letter, a pair of spectacles, writing apparatus, and so on, are painted on the table as if they really lay there. The point of these additions is the jest of deceiving the eye through the realism of the painting. In the seventeenth century this table was still a far-famed work; later on it fell into oblivion,

Fig. 10. A SCHOOLMASTER'S SIGN-BOARD. Oil-painting of 1516.
In the Basle Museum.

and was only rediscovered in the year 1871, unfortunately in a badly damaged condition.

In the year 1515 Holbein also appeared as a portrait-painter. The Darmstadt Museum possesses the bust, half life-size, of a young man, signed with this date and the initials H.H. The unknown youth is dressed in scarlet cloth; a cap of the same material is placed on his fair hair; the background is a light sky-blue. The young painter has tested his skill in colouring by a bold experiment — and he has succeeded well (Fig. 6).

In another piece of work by Holbein of the same year, quite unique in its kind, we recognise him as a master of rapid invention and execution. This is his series of marginal drawings to the "Praise of Folly" by Erasmus

of Rotterdam. Erasmus had come to Basle in the year 1513 for the first
time in order to treat with the famous printer, Johannes Froben, for the
publication of his collection of adages and his edition of the New Testament.
Since then the renowned scholar had spent a considerable part of each year
at Basle. Froben published also in 1514 the keenly satirical book, "En-
comion Morias" (Praise of Folly), which was written in the Latin language,

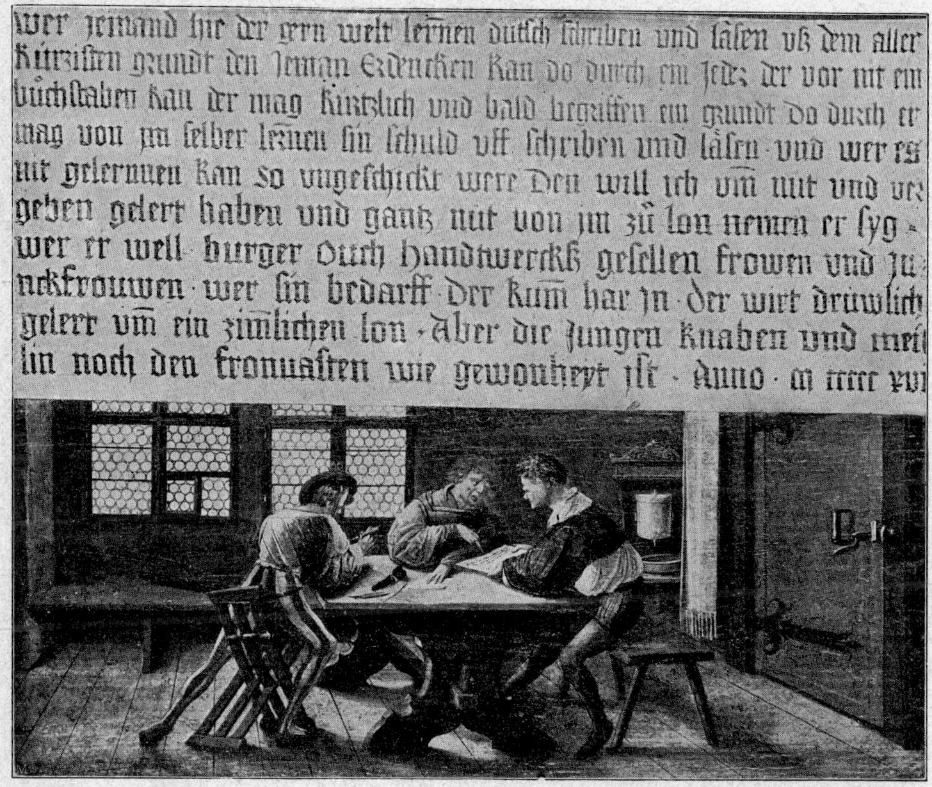

Fig. 11. A SCHOOLMASTER'S SIGN-BOARD. Oil-painting of 1516.
In the Basle Museum.

but in a popular vein. In a copy of this book destined for the author's private
use Holbein drew eighty-two little pictures on the margins, about two inches
wide. He carried out this piece of work, as we are informed in a note
entered on the title-page, in the space of ten days, for the delectation of
Erasmus. From another note we learn that these illustrations were produced
towards the end of the year 1515. It remains unknown whether they owe
their origin to a wish of Erasmus himself or whether a friend ordered them
as a present for him. The precious book is now among the treasures of
the Holbein collection in the Basle Museum. The drawings, thrown off
with the pen in quick and easy strokes without long reflection, illustrate
wittily and with sound humour the adjacent passages of the text or

Fig. 12. THE BURGOMASTER JAKOB MEYER. Drawing in silver-point and red chalk.
In the Basle Museum.
(After an original photograph by Braun, Clément & Co., Dornach (Alsace) and Paris.)

the explanatory glosses on the margin. The introduction is a picture of "Moria" (Folly), in the shape of a young woman wearing a fool's cap and bells, who mounts the teacher's chair to pronounce a panegyric on herself. Then the draughtsman has drawn from the text and the marginal notes with the most extreme variety whatever appeared to him adapted to pictorial treatment. His fancies do not always go to the root of the matter; frequently a mere phrase of casual occurrence has given him the suggestion for a drawing: for instance, at a place where the proverbial expression is employed "to understand as much about a thing as an ass does about lute-playing", he has drawn an ass standing with a delighted expression on its face opposite to an aristocratic harp-player and accompanying his music with its own melodious voice. The explanations contained in the glosses of the mythological allusions which occur in the text have especially instigated him to mischievous and playful designs which place the legends of the Gods in a ridiculous light. A telling instance of the vivacity of spirit with which Holbein found subjects for pictures in the words is the drawing for a passage in which the medieval theologian Nicolaus de Lyra is mentioned; here the mere name was sufficient to suggest to him an idea for a picture: the pious and learned man sits by the side of his desk with a hurdy-gurdy.

Once Erasmus mentions his own name in the text. Here Holbein has drawn him, too, on the margin, sitting in his study, and has written the name Erasmus in larger letters as well. The little picture contains nothing malicious, but the scholar has nevertheless revenged himself on the young artist for the jest of introducing the portrait of his own person among the caricatures: on the following page beside the drawing of a fat voluptuary, who practises the doctrines of Epicurus as regards women and wine, is written the name of Holbein in the hand of Erasmus. It is not necessary to conclude from this playful tit-for-tat that the young Holbein was a notorious rake; what it does show is that between the two men, one of whom stood at the height of his fame while the other was still only on the threshold of his career, there were already friendly relations from which the young artist could not fail to derive great honour. The large majority of the marginal drawings, of course, relate to the follies themselves, to which men of all ranks are liable, and in these pictorial mockeries of human self-conceit the artist shows himself a match for the author of the satire in going to the point. The concluding picture shows us Moria herself once more, descending from the chair after saying farewell to the audience, who follow her steps with faces of the most varied expression (Fig 7). The most surprising thing in all these slight little drawings, next to their spontaneity and sprightliness, is the sharpness with which character is expressed in so few strokes.

Holbein, doubtless, owed his acquaintance with Erasmus to the printer Froben. This celebrated publisher gave employment to the young artist soon

Fig. 13. DOROTHEA KANNENGIESSER, WIFE OF THE BURGOMASTER JAKOB MEYER.
Drawing in silver-point and red chalk.
In the Basle Museum.
(After an original photograph by Braun, Clément & Co., Dornach (Alsace)
and Paris.)

after his arrival at Basle by setting him to draw designs on wood for the decoration of printed books. A title-border signed with Hans Holbein's name, consisting of a Renaissance arch enlivened with children, with tritons represented as if in a relief on the base, occurs in the editions of several books of 1515 and the following years. Then there follow, from 1516 onwards, various borders in which subjects with figures play the principal part: the histories of Mucius Scaevola, Marcus Curtius, and Cleopatra, the myth of

Fig. 14. THE BURGOMASTER JAKOB MAYER. Oil-painting of 1516.
In the Basle Museum.
(After an original photograph by Braun, Clément & Co., Dornach (Alsace) and Paris.)

Tantalus and Pelops (Fig. 8) and other classical stories which had obtained a new lease of life in that period of humanism, are brought before the spectator. It is noticeable that Holbein has here already made use of antique costume, the knowledge of which he derived from the engravings of Mantegna, instead of the dress of his own time. Then there is a title-border with the illustrations of the power of women, which had been so popular since the Middle Ages: Paris, Pyramus, David and Solomon are introduced as examples of men in subjection to women. Besides complete title-borders, Holbein also designed single side-pieces, alphabets adorned with figures and single letters for printed books; he further designed publishers' devices to be placed on the title or at the conclusion of the book, not only for Froben but for other printers. The publisher's mark of Johannes Froben was a caduceus held by two hands, on the knob of which, between the heads of the two snakes, a dove is sitting. In the large book-plate (ex-libris) of Froben (Fig. 9) we see this device placed on a shield supported by children within a rich Renaissance arch; the prettily

Fig. 15. THE WIFE OF THE BURGOMASTER JAKOB MEYER. Oil-painting of 1516.
In the Basle Museum.
(After an original photograph by Braun, Clément & Co., Dornach (Alsace) and Paris).

designed print is unfortunately disfigured by defective cutting. The cutting of these early drawings on wood by Holbein is, generally speaking, very imperfect: the line drawn by the artist's hand often appears sadly spoilt. In the case of several of the prints which are not signed with a name it remains doubtful whether Hans Holbein or his brother Ambrosius, who worked in the same field, was the author. Froben's device was also carried out by Hans Holbein on a larger scale, as a picture, so to speak, in tempera, on canvas. This design, which is in the collection of drawings at the Basle Museum, is a pattern of good taste; in its clear, simple drawing, sketched out in a few tones, it produces the most excellent decorative effect. The staff with the snakes and dove, held by hands emerging from clouds, hangs in light colours in front of a dark-blue ground, under an arch resting on short pillars with capitals of the Corinthian type and shafts, dark-red with spaces left for the lights, which give the impression of highly polished marble.

The young painter accepted every commission which was offered to him. Thus in 1516 he painted a signboard for a schoolmaster (Fig. 10 and 11). This was a board to be hung up outside the school-house and looked at from both sides; each side consequently received an inscription and a picture. The board, split into halves to show the two sides, is now in the Basle Museum. The inscription, expressed in the same terms on both sides, promises to all who desire to learn reading and writing in German, be they citizen or apprentice, wife or maid, to teach it them

Fig. 16. ADAM AND EVE. Painting in oils on paper, 1517.
In the Basle Museum.

thoroughly in the shortest space of time, on the condition of accepting no
fee from anyone in whose case the instruction has proved to be fruitless.
It also announces the usual school-term for young boys and girls. All this,
expressed at length, occupies the greater part of the area of the board.
To enliven this appeal to the passers-by with pictures, a long narrow space
at the bottom on each side remained free. Here Holbein painted, without
much outlay of artistic power, as was to be expected, but still with pleasure
in the painting and in a cheerful mood, two pleasing little pictures in which
he represents on one side the instruction of the children and on the other
that of the adults. In the first we look into a bare room with a floor of
boards and grey plastered walls. By the wall on the long side of the
room, under the casements with leaded panes, stands a simple bench; a
second bench stands just in the centre of the room; to left and right is
a desk on either side. At one desk the schoolmaster sits on a box, dressed
in red and yellow, with a red cap on his head: he gives a friendly touch
with the rod to a reading boy in a green jacket. Opposite sits the school-
dame, in a red dress and white coif, on a chair, engaged in teaching a girl
dressed in blue and green. In the middle two boys sit, one on the bench,

the other on a stool which stands near it, reading to themselves, one dressed in blue, the other in yellow, with a red cap. The little picture, quite unpretending as it is, has the charm of perfect naïveté; the expression, not only in the faces but also in the gestures, is quite excellent. The other little picture possesses still more charm as a painting. The natural illumination, with the light falling through the windows from behind upon the figures and the slanting shadow which spreads out towards the front,

Fig. 17. STUDY FROM NATURE.
Silver-point and water-colour drawing.
In the Basle Museum.
(After an original photograph by Braun, Clément & Co.,
Dornach (Alsace) and Paris.)

is conveyed without ambiguity. The room here is like the other, but looks rather more home-like. On the wall we see a washing-apparatus with a clean towel. In the middle stands a table with chairs. There sits the schoolmaster, now facing exactly to the front — this is, doubtless, a portrait — in the same costume as before, between two grown-up young men, dressed in the Landsknecht fashion, one in stripes of red and yellow, the other in green. The expression of the faces is again masterly; the look of the man in green, especially, who is exerting himself with the utmost pains to take in what the teacher says to him, is unspeakably comic.

But, besides such modest tasks of slight execution, Holbein was also painting portraits in which he satisfied the highest claims which can be made upon an artist, by evincing his mastery of the art of making a true picture, a harmonious work of art in form and colour, complete in itself, out of the life-like portrait of a man, and by carrying out his work with the utmost technical accomplishment. In this very year (1516) the newly-elected Burgomaster of Basle, Jakob Meyer, gave him a commission to paint himself and his wife. The Basle Museum possesses not only the portraits of husband and wife united in one frame, but also the preliminary studies which Holbein made for them. These consist of drawings of the heads, carried out with the most extreme care and delicacy on the same scale in which they were to appear in the painting —

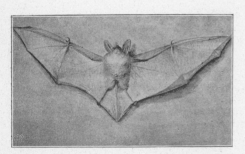

Fig. 18. STUDY FROM NATURE. Silver-point and water-colour drawing. In the Basle Museum.
(After an original photograph by Braun, Clément & Co.,
Dornach (Alsace) and Paris.)

Fig. 19. THE LAST SUPPER. Oil-painting in the Basle Museum.
(After an original photograph by Braun, Clément & Co., Dornach (Alsace) and Paris.)

half the size of life. The artist determined the outlines with the silver-
point, in lines as thin as a hair, which are as clear and definite as the
strokes of a pen; with the same point he gave roundness to the forms by
light and delicate modelling, and rendered with great precision the different
qualities of the skin according as it lies on hard or soft parts of the face:
then he touched in the redder portions of the skin with red chalk. The
drawing of the man's head, in particular, is so thoroughly carried out that
this preliminary study for a picture has all the value of an independent
work of art. Jakob Meyer, with the additional surname "Zum Hasen"

(at the sign of the hare) — such distinguishing sur names were derived from the sign of the person's house — reveals himself to us as a dignified personality, in whose features kindness and decision are united. Thus, we can form a good idea of the man, who, after going through several campaigns in Italy, was the first man of plebeian descent to be called to take the lead in the government of Basle, where he carried out with caution and energy, during a series of successive years

Fig. 20. BONIFACIUS AMERBACH. Oil-painting in the Basle Museum.
Inscription:
Though but a painted face, I yield not to the living features of my master, but in true lineaments I am a noble likeness of him. Whilst he brings for the eighth time a space of three years to its close, art thus expresses skilfully in me to hat nature has made him.
Johannes Holbein painted Bonifacius Amerbach, 14th October, 1519.
(After an original photograph by Braun, Clément & Co., Dornach (Alsace) and Paris.)

of office, far-reaching innovations in the constitution of the town (Fig. 12). The wife of the Burgomaster, Dorothea Kannegiesser, appears young and pretty; she was Jakob Meyer's second wife, whom he had led home but a few years before (Fig. 13). After Holbein had made such preparatory drawings, in which form and expression were already completely fixed, he was able in carrying out the painting to direct his whole attention to the colour. Even for the sake of the colour, he had no need to weary his model by numerous and lengthy sittings. On the portrait drawing of Jakob Meyer we see in the left upper corner some observations in writing in Holbein's hand; these are notes on the colour, for instance: "eye-brows lighter than the hair". Hence we perceive that the artist had the intention, which he doubtless carried out, when he painted the pictures, to rely on his memory for colours, supported, in case of need, by such notes as these, and to translate the drawings into paintings as far as possible out of his own head. Holbein kept up this practice throughout his life. A portrait of a lady in the Basle Museum, which remained unfinished at an early stage of the work, affords an interesting glimpse of his method in painting; the drawing is precise and within it all the colors are laid on in perfectly flat tones, the flesh only being slightly modelled from the first. The painted double-portrait of the Meyer couple (Fig. 14 and 15) is a work of remarkable merit. Holbein had caught from his father a liking for the invention of architecture in the new Italian taste, in the style of the Renaissance. He has, accordingly, placed the two busts in an architectural frame of this kind, the creation of his own fancy. It is conceived as a consecutive whole through the two halves of the picture. It

Fig. 21. SUPPOSED PORTRAIT OF HOLBEIN HIMSELF.
Drawing in coloured chalks in the Basle Museum.

introduces variety of form and colour into the background; the grey stone is variegated and enlivened by reddish-brown marble columns with gold decorations and by dark-blue tones in the compartments of the vault. In the man's portrait there is a narrow outlook on the light-blue sky, and in the woman's a broad one. Jakob Meyer wears a black coat, a white shirt with gold embroidery on the border and a scarlet cap on his curly, brown hair; the red and the sky-blue stand side by side, just as in the portrait in the Darmstadt Museum, painted a year before. The portrait of the wife is, if possible, still more splendid in colour than that of the husband. Head and neck stand out against the blue sky in the light flesh-tones of a blonde, the cool colouring of which is set off still further by a warm tone in the white fabric, embroidered with gold ornaments, by the head-dress and bodice; a couple of slender chains on the white neck, and glittering metallic ornaments on the border of the bodice enliven the mass of light colour, which is sharply marked off at the bottom by the wide black velvet trimming of the scarlet dress.

A small picture dated 1517 in the Basle Museum shows Adam and Eve as busts (Fig. 16). It is a painstaking study from nature painted in oil-colours

Fig. 22. MADONNA. Washed drawing, a design for glass-painting. Basle Museum.

on paper, the charm of which as a painting consists in the contrasted effect of light and dark flesh — Adam is dark-complexioned, Eve a blonde — side by side on the black background.

Fig. 23. St. Anne with the Virgin Mary and the infant Jesus.
Washed design for glass-painting. In the Basle Museum.
(After an original photograph by Braun, Clément & Co., Dornach (Alsace)
and Paris.)

A pair of pretty little drawings in the Basle Museum bears witness to Holbein's thoroughness in studying nature, even in trifles. In one we see a lamb and a lamb's head, drawn with exquisite delicacy and carried out so as to give the full effect of paintings, by a very slight application of water-colours (Fig. 17). On the other a bat spread out is drawn with the same care; the veins, which are seen through the transparent membrane of the wings, are gone over with red water-colour, and it is wonderful what a picturesque and coloured effect is produced by this means and by the slight touching-up of a few other places with the reddish tone (Fig. 18).

In the year 1517 Holbein visited Lucerne. Here a task of considerable extent in the way of wall-painting awaited him.

Whilst in the rest of Germany at that time few opportunities were offered to painters of displaying their art in this special field, to which their Italian contemporaries owed in an eminent degree the freedom and largeness of their style, the German towns in the neighbourhood of the Alpine barrier — in the first instance probably Augsburg, which was the chief promoter of intercourse with Italy — had adopted the North Italian custom of decorating the exterior of houses with paintings instead of seeking means to enliven their surfaces by the use of Gothic decorative forms; the walls were left perfectly plain in order to receive such decoration, and the windows received a simple, rectangular shape at an early date. The painting of the inner rooms of middle-class houses with figurative subjects had already been popular for more than a century in this region.

Holbein had, accordingly, to decorate the house of the magistrate, Jakob von Hertenstein, at Lucerne with paintings within and without. In the interior, religious subjects were represented in one chamber and genre-subjects in others; also the fable of the foun-

Fig. 24. St. Barbara. Washed design for glass-painting. In the Basle Museum. (After an original photograph by Braun, Clément & Co., Dornach (Alsace) and Paris.)

tain of youth, whose water restores youthful vigour and beauty to the old and decrepit. On the outside a place was found for historical pictures; the material for these, at this time when everyone had taken to the study of classical antiquity, was no longer taken from the medieval poems, but from the history of the Greeks and Romans, mingled, it is true, with later legends.

The Hertenstein house was standing, with its decorative paintings still in great part well preserved, till the year 1824; then it had to be pulled down, and there are only very inadequate copies, apart from a few remains hardly worth mentioning and a small washed sketch for one of the paintings,

Fig. 25. ST. CATHERINE. Washed design for a painted window.
In the Basle Museum.
(After an original photograph by Braun, Clément & Co., Dornach (Alsace)
and Paris.)

to preserve the memory of Holbein's first monumental achievement. For all that, we can still form from the copies some idea of the external decoration of the house; if not of the beauty of detail, yet, at least, of the tastefulness of the general scheme. The ground-floor was left without ornament. On the principal storey, where numerous windows close together left little space, the painting was confined to three single female figures, one at each corner and one on the broad space between the windows in the middle. Over these one saw to the left ornaments with

figures, adapted to the irregular headings of the windows, and to the right, where the windows stood in a straight line, a frieze of children fighting. Between these subjects, painted in grisaille, there was a larger picture in colours in the middle, the upper part of which extended to the second storey. This picture broke the surface of the wall in such a way that it looked as if a semicircular bay projected from the wall, and one looked through its wide, arched opening into an inner room; this inner room was chosen as the scene of a picture, the subject of which was taken from the legend of the three princes who have to prove before the corpse of the old king which of them is his true-born son. To right and left between the windows the heraldic emblems of matrimonial alliances, framed in wreathed arches, were introduced. In the space between the windows of the second floor and those of the third there was a triumphal procession, divided into single groups by pilasters, and placed on a base-line which took no notice of the unequal height of the windows. Holbein had borrowed these groups from the engravings of Andrea Mantegna, "the Triumph of Caesar"; true to his original, he had here introduced antique costumes, whilst in the other historical pictures of the façade he still clothed the figures in the costume of his own time. The pictures between the windows on the third storey, which extended to the cornice of the roof, showed examples

Fig. 26. FIGURE OF THE VIRGIN, WITH A DONOR. Washed design for a painted window. In the Basle Museum.
(After an original photograph by Braun, Clément & Co., Dornach (Alsace) and Paris.)

of antique magnanimity; the rejection of the teacherous schoolmaster of
Falerii, the Athenian Leaena, who bit off her tongue that she might not
be able to denounce her lover before the tribunal, Mucius Scaevola before
Porsenna, the suicide of
Lucretia and the self-
sacrifice of Marcus Cur-
tius. In the last-named
picture the Roman knight
was represented as if he
were urging on his
horse to leap down into
the street. The con-
stancy of Leaena is that
one of the paintings of
which an original sketch
is preserved; in this
drawing (in the Basle
Museum) we see the
story, so difficult to represent in a picture,
told as clearly as was
possible, with a few
figures, and the irregu-
lar space ably filled by
the architecture of the
judgment-hall.

It is possible that
Holbein made an excur-
sion from Lucerne across
the Italian frontier. It is
true that an early bio-
grapher expressly states
that he was never in
Italy. But that does
not prevent his having
visited Milan, which lay
so near to Switzerland.
What suggests it is the
circumstance that Hol-

Fig. 27. THE ARCHANGEL MICHAEL.
Washed design for a painted window. In the Basle Museum.
(After an original photograph by Braun, Clément & Co., Dornach (Alsace)
and Paris.)

bein painted a Last Supper which presents great and unmistakeable re-
semblances to the celebrated fresco of Leonardo da Vinci in Santa Maria
delle Grazie at Milan. The picture, of which the side portions are wanting,
is in the Basle Museum. In Amerbach's time it was already damaged and
badly restored; at a later date it was again restored and repainted in a hard
and gaudy way, so that one can hardly form any idea of the original scheme

of colour. All that one can still appreciate is the vigorous and telling expression of the heads. The composition, the figure of the Saviour and the whole

Fig. 28. CHRIST BEFORE CAIAPHAS. From the series of washed drawings of the Passion of Christ (designs for glass-paintings) in the Basle Museum.

movement which passes through the group remind us so strongly of Leonardo's master-piece, that we are bound to assume that Holbein had seen it (Fig. 19).

On returning to Basle Holbein was admitted to the painter's guild of that place, on 25th September 1519.

Fig. 29. THE SCOURGING. From the series of washed drawings of the Passion of Christ (designs for glass-paintings) in the Basle Museum. (After an original photograph by Braun, Clément & Co., Dornach (Alsace) and Paris.)

A few weeks later he finished a master-piece of portrait-painting, the bust of Bonifacius Amerbach. This learned and artistic man, distinguished also for his great personal charm, who at a later time collected all of Holbein's works that he could lay hands on and whose portrait found its way with this whole collection to the Basle Museum, reveals himself here in such a speaking and life-like presentment, that we acknowledge without the least doubt the justice of the verses which he composed for the picture, praising the excellence of the likeness. The colour-scheme of the picture is remarkable. The fine head, of a warm complexion and with reddish-brown hair and beard, stands out from a dark-blue sky; the sitter wears a black robe trimmed with black fur, under which a waistcoat of light blue damask and a white linen collar can be seen. The blue of the sky is slightly relieved by a distant view of snowy mountains, while it is firmly limited and intersected by the warm brown and green tones of the stem and branches of a fig-tree. On the stem of the tree hangs in a wooden frame the parchment sheet with the inscription, which contains besides the aforesaid verses the names of the painter and of the person represented, together with the date (14th October 1519) (Fig. 20).

On 3rd July 1520
Holbein took the
oath as a citizen
of the town of
Basle. Probably
about the same
time he married
Elsbeth, a widow.
The status of a
citizen and mar-
riage were pre-
sumably required
by the regulations
of the guilds of
Basle (as expressly
as by those of
other towns), from
everyone who
wished to settle
there as a master.

We can form
an idea of the
young master's
appearance from
the fine drawing in
coloured crayons
in the Basle Mu-
seum, which passes
as his portrait of
himself (Fig. 21).
It ought, however,

Fig. 30. THE MOCKING OF CHRIST. From the series of washed drawings of the
Passion (designs for glass-paintings) in the Basle Museum.

to be mentioned that the correctness of this designation is not beyond
dispute. The old Amerbach catalogue calls this picture a "counterfeit
of Holbein with dry colours", and from these words it is not positively
to be concluded that it is a "counterfeit" of himself. Points of likeness
to the portraits of him as a child done by his father are, indeed, to be
found; but the resemblance between a child and a grown-up man is always
somewhat indefinite and remote. But whether the portrait represents the
master himself or some other person it is, at any rate, a work of eminent
merit. The execution is extraordinarily finished, quite in a painter's
manner. The drawing was done with black chalk and the various tones
of coloured crayons are rubbed in so lightly and neatly that they produce
the impression of water-colour. In the face alone coloured tones are also
drawn in lines with a pointed crayon. His intelligent face, with the clear,
brown eyes, may well be that of the painter who quietly and surely

Fig. 31. PILATE WASHING HIS HANDS. From the series of washed drawings of the Passion (designs for glass-paintings) in the Basle Museum.

observed the outer world and was full of creative energy within. On the short, dark-brown hair rests a red hat with a wide brim. The color of the coat, trimmed with black velvet, is a light, brownish grey. On the

Fig. 32. CHRIST BEARING THE CROSS. From the series of washed drawings of the Passion (designs for glass-paintings) in the Basle Museum.

(After an original photograph by Braun, Clément & Co., Dornach (Alsace) and Paris.)

Fig. 33. THE CRUCIFIXION. From the series of washed drawings of the Passion (designs for glass-painting)
in the Basle Museum.
(After an original photograph by Braun, Clément & Co., Dornach (Alsace) and Paris.)

shirt, which is visible at the neck, the lights are put on with white. For the hardness of general outline, which somewhat takes from the picturesque effect of the splendid portrait, the artist is not responsible; the figure was subsequently cut out along the contours, and mounted on grey paper.

Fig. 34. THE ARMS OF THE HOLDERMEIER FAMILY, design for a painted window.
Washed drawing of the year 1518. In the Basle Museum.
(After an original photograph by Braun, Clément & Co., Dornach (Alsace) and Paris.)

For seven years after his reception into the guild Holbein remained at Basle without interrupting his sojourn for any length of time, and displayed an abundant industry.

The best general impression of his many-sided productiveness is to be gathered from the precious collection of drawings which belongs to the

3*

Fig. 35. DESIGN FOR AN ARMORIAL WINDOW. Washed drawing
in the Basle Museum.

Basle Museum and of which by far the greatest part is derived from the collection started by Bonifacius Amerbach and considerably increased by his son Basilius, which the town of Basle purchased in 1661 as "a rare jewel".

There we find those exquisite portrait-drawings which give a speaking resemblance to life and the full effect of a picture in a way that is perfectly unique, and this by the very simplest means: just an outline and a few tints rubbed in, or put in with the brush; we find, too, studies of other kinds, drawings which are complete works of art in themselves, designs for larger works and patterns for various branches of decorative art.

Among these last the so-called "Scheibenrisse", i. e. designs for paintings on glass, take the first place as regards number.

Glass-painting had long lost the pre-eminence which it once enjoyed among the various branches of the painter's art; at the Renaissance it fell into complete dependence on easel-painting. It surrendered the tapestry-like quality which had characterized it, and managed, by the aid of newly invented processes, to rival the new painting in plastic modelling and the effects of perspective. It ceased also to be a purely ecclesiastical art; it adorned single panes in the otherwise uncoloured windows of private houses with armorial bearings and figure-subjects. Here the pictures were placed before the eyes of the spectator at a very short distance, and a rich painting on a smale scale was developed in a narrow space upon a framework of leading, which was reduced to the lowest possible proportions; the nicest and most delicate execution was therefore indispensable. It was natural that when such wholly different demands were made upon them the glasiers should like to have the designs for their work prepared for them by painters of another branch of the art.

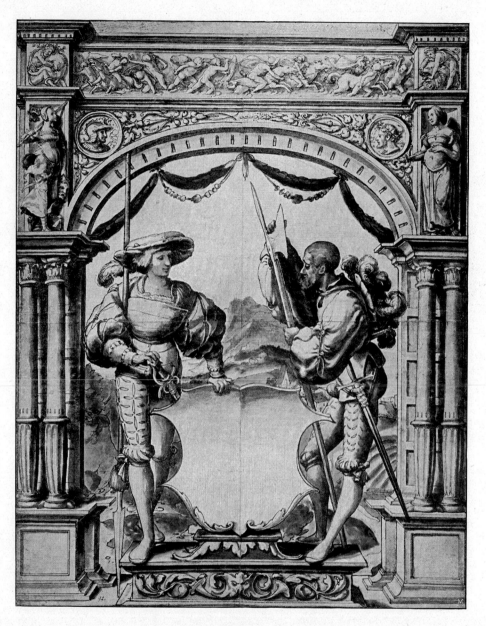

Fig. 36. DESIGN FOR A PAINTED WINDOW. Washed drawing with indications of colour.
In the Royal Print - Cabinet, Berlin.

Holbein prepared designs for heraldic glass as well as religious subjects for windows. These are all wash-drawings done with the brush on the scale of the glass-paintings themselves, with vigorous suggestions of the effects of light and shade. In this way the drawing of the outlines and all that had to be expressed by the leading was settled for the glasier exactly, but the choice of colours was left to his taste; only in single cases did Holbein think it advisable to indicate his ideas for the colours by a few slight tints. The first requisite in

Fig. 37. DESIGN FOR AN ARMORIAL WINDOW.
Washed drawing in the Basle Museum.

work of this kind was decorative effect; the well-arranged distribution of forms over the surface which they were intended to adorn. The earliest of these designs for glass-painting by Holbein are several pictures of Saints. In the figures which we see in these pictures a singular blemish, which is frequently observable in Holbein's earlier works, strikes the eye in a peculiarly disagreeable way. The legs of almost all the figures are much too short. But we also have the impression that in making these designs the artist hardly bestowed so much attention upon the figures as upon their surroundings, in which he designed rich and fantastic Renaissance architecture with inexhaustible power of imagination. Sometimes this architectural structure forms a border to frame in the figure, which stands by itself; sometimes it retires towards the back of the picture and forms a shrine shaped like an archway; or it is prolonged, as if forming part of a large edifice, into the space behind the figures, filled in other cases by a distant landscape. These last and richest architectural forms,

Fig. 38. DESIGN FOR THE ARMS OF A BISHOP. Washed drawing for painted glass.
In the Basle Museum.
(After an original photograph by Braun, Clément & Co., Dornach (Alsace) and Paris.)

which gave an opportunity for the most varied developments in the composition of fanciful buildings, are to be found in a connected series of
eight designs for panes of glass (from which Fig. 22—25 are selected)
which are so applied that every two pictures are planned to form a pair,
placed in the two compartments of a window, and there is, consequently,

Fig. 39. THE ARMS OF BASLE. Washed drawing slightly tinted with water-colours, for a glass-painting.
In the Basle Museum.
(After an original photograph by Braun, Clément & Co., Dornach (Alsace) and Paris.)

a correspondence and symmetry in the architecture of the two, without
their agreeing exactly in details (Fig. 23 and 24). If one can infer the date
of the compositions from the greater prominence of the already mentioned
blemish in the figures these eight designs for windows must be the oldest
of all. In the case of a single picture of the Virgin the circumstance that the
landscape in the background gives a view of the town of Lucerne is a
reason for supposing that the picture was produced during Holbein's stay

Numine uirgo tuum pleno defende Friburgum
Inferni noceant ne mala fpectra Iouis.
Tecu tuis Lamberte aris oftende patronum,
Turba Paleftinum fentiat omnis herum.

Fig. 40. THE PATRON SAINTS OF FREIBURG. Woodcut on the back of the title-
page of "Stadtrechte und Statuten der löblichen Stadt Freiburg im Breisgau",
by Ulrich Zasius, published in 1520.
　　Inscription below:
　　　　Defend Freiburg, o Virgin, by thy mighty power,
　　　　that no evil spirits of the Prince of Hell may do it harm;
　　　　and do thou, Lambert, show thyself the Patron of thine own altars;
　　　　may the knight of Palestine appal the hosts of the enemy.

in that town. In a very fine design for glass-painting, which, to judge from the good proportions of the figures, belongs to a later time, the Virgin, a charming figure, who contemplates the child in her arms with a loving expression on her face, stands in front of a niche, shut off by pillars, the beautiful architecture of which is much simpler in taste than is usual in Holbein's early works; the figure of the Virgin is conceived as a piece of sculpture; she stands on an ornamented base, and the rays which surround her from head to foot as a symbol, current in art, of the immaculate conception, appear to be made of metal.

The donor of the picture kneels on one side in the costume of a knight, with the expression of fervent supplication in his face and in his outspread hands (Fig. 26). In contrast to this comparatively quiet architecture, which serves admirably by its well-balanced masses to give prominence to the figure in the middle, we find the utmost vagaries of fantastic architecture in a drawing which represents Christ on the cross between the Virgin and St. John. The structural forms of the framework go off into mere ornaments, and the luxuriant play of Holbein's Renaissance ornament reacts upon the lines and even upon the expression of countenance of the figures.

In a rich composition which represents the Coronation of the Virgin as Queen of Heaven Holbein has left out the architectural frame completely and displayed his liking for the creation of fanciful masonry only in the splendid throne standing on the clouds, on which the figures of God the Father and God the Son are seated. Another design with-

Fig. 41. Design for a portion of a painted façade, with the figure of Charlemagne. Washed drawing in the Basle Museum.
(After an original photograph by Braun, Clément & Co., Dornach (Alsace) and Paris.)

out a frame is a particularly fine one of the Archangel Michael, who is conceived as a figure carved in wood, standing on a kind of bracket; the angel holds the scales of judgment and weighs the burden of sin, suggested by the figure of a devil, against the power of redemption, symbolized by the child Christ (Fig. 27). A unique position, in respect of subject, among the designs for glass-painting is held by an excellent drawing, which shows the prodigal son as a swineherd within a frame-border. In a landscape closed in by mountains the herd of swine is gathered round an oak-tree, and their keeper, as if urged by unrest within, steps quickly forward, with the shy look of a man who has gone wrong, but on whose features such a feeling of misery is stamped that the sight of him awakens compassion rather than abhorrence.

The most important, as regards their contents, of all the designs for glass-painting by Holbein which are extant, are the series of ten subjects from the Passion of Christ. Here, too, the artist has given free play to his delight in the invention of rich and powerful forms, structural and ornamental, in "antique" taste. But he has laid the chief stress after all on the figure-subjects, which occupy the interior of these frames, as perfect master-pieces of the art of filling a space. Even if we do not find in these compositions the unapproachable depth of feeling and the impressive poetry of Dürer, they make for all that a more immediate appeal to the understanding and the feeling of the modern spectator owing to the remarkably lucid and natural representation of the incidents — conceived more from the dramatic than from the religious standpoint — and by the simple and natural beauty of

Fig. 42. LADY OF BASLE IN A RICH DRESS AND HAT WITH FEATHERS.
Washed drawing in the Basle Museum.

the forms, which avoid all hardness. A subordinate circumstance also tells
—that there is nowhere any intrusion of contemporary costume, and that
the figures of warriors, especially, are for the most part arrayed in the antique
Roman dress, after Mantegna's pattern. It is not to be denied that this
effort after historical accuracy even in externals, this removal of the action
to a far distant past, must have involved for the great majority of contemporary beholders a certain sacrifice of effectiveness to touch the heart,
by comparison with the impression which the works of the earlier masters
made, by treating the events of the Saviour's life as the doings of God

Fig. 43. LADY OF BASLE IN A CLOTH DRESS AND EMBROIDERED CAP.
Washed drawing in the Basle Museum. (After an original photograph by Braun,
Clément & Co., Dornach (Alsace) and Paris).

for all time and adapting them to their own era. The series begins with Christ being led before Caiaphas. We have a side-view of the throne of the High-Priest, which is erected in a richly decorated hall. Fronting him stands the Saviour in bonds, turning his head with a wonderfully expressive look of questioning and of innocence to the man-at-arms, who has struck him with his fist (Fig. 28). The Scourging, too, is placed in a splendid room, and the artist's love of design has given ornaments to the very column of martyrdom. Christ leans against the column powerless, with his arms

Fig. 44. CITIZEN'S WIFE OF BASLE. Washed drawing in the Basle Museum.

tied and with sunken head, at the mercy of the blows of three executioners
and under the observation of a person in authority. In the figures of the
executioners it is noticeable that they do not possess that fulness of life
which Holbein was usually able to give to figures in violent movement
(Fig. 29). All the more vigorous and impressive is the treatment of the
mocking of Christ, the scene of which is a hall designed, by way of exception,
in the Gothic style (Fig. 30). The following picture represents the placing
of the crown of thorns. We look from the side on the Saviour seated on
a chair. One of the soldiers kneels in mockery before him, whilst another
offers him the reed as a sceptre; two others force the crown upon his head

with a staff, and a third strikes the head with a stick. Behind the seat
stands Pilate as a spectator with the judge's wand in his hand. In this
case the border, which consists of a pair of pillars
united at the top by ornaments, is not suffered
to have any connexion with the architecture of
the room, but surrounds the whole as a detached
frame. In all the following drawings, too, the
frames form merely an external finish having no
essential connexion with the picture. Such an
arrangement was demanded here by the fact that
the action takes place in the open air; this limi-
tation of the architectural accessories, however,
did not prevent Holbein from giving play even
here to the richness of his imagination in the
utmost variety. In the subject which follows the
crowning with thorns, the picture of a town opens
before us. We look on the open place before
the hall of judgment. A tumultuous populace, so
skilfully suggested by the artist that a few figures
produce the effect of a great multitude, fills the
square. Their outcry is the response to the words
of contemptuous pity, accompanied by a lively
play of feature and gesture, with which Pilate
presents to the people the patient sufferer who
stands beside him with downcast looks. In the
next picture we see the governor's throne, with
a canopied roof, erected in a spacious inner court.
With an expression of great resolution Pilate carries
out the symbolical action of washing his hands,
whilst he pronounces a last utterance and gazes
after the throng which leads away Christ, abandoned
to its mercy. Christ walks in the foreground in
the midst of a crowd of soldiers, and his eye is
fixed in silent questioning upon a man in armour,
whose iron fist grasps his arm (Fig. 31). Then
follows the bearing of the cross. A dense throng
of men passes through the town-gate, which
affords a small glimpse into the street, whilst a
piece of the town-wall, guarded by a tower, appears
outside. At the head of the procession walk
the two thieves, tied with cords. Christ follows
them, his knees just giving way under the burden

Fig. 45. Christ in the tomb. Oil-painting of 1521. In the Basle Museum.

of the cross. An officer of the soldiery, who walks by his side, seizes
him by the shoulder with reproaches and threats; the men push him
and strike him. Over the heads of the figures arms and implements

project and in this way the impression of a numerous crowd is effectively
heightened (Fig. 32). The next subject represents in a vigorous and impressive composition the preparations for the Crucifixion. Christ kneels on
the cross, which lies on the ground. Two executioners strip him by violently
drawing off his tunic over his head. In front a man is busily engaged in
boring holes for the nails in the transverse beam of the cross. Another is
digging out the hole in which the cross is to be planted. In the background
we see a multitude of people, among them one of the thieves, who is
already stripped. Next to the subject of the stripping of Christ is that in
which he is nailed to the cross. This action is also depicted with great

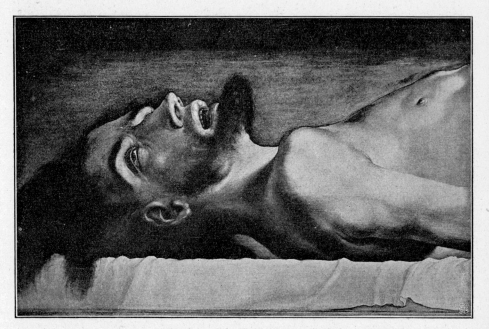

Fig. 46. HEAD OF THE PICTURE OF A DEAD MAN IN THE BASLE MUSEUM (see preceding fig.).
(After an original photograph by Braun, Clément & Co., Dornach (Alsace) and Paris.

vivacity. The professional roughness ot the hangman is expressed crudely
but without exaggeration. An officer of justice in cap and fur and a high
official in oriental attire riding on a mule look on coolly and without emotion.
In the middle distance we see the soldiers throwing dice for Christ's coat,
and, farther back, a great crowd of people. In the last picture we see the
three crosses erected. Christ turns his head aside and down towards his
mother, who supported by St. John, has made her way close to the stem
of the cross, but cannot bear to look up. A man, who has fastened up
the placard with the inscription, steps down the ladder at the back of the
cross. We see the sponge with vinegar stuck upon a pole. In front of
the soldiers, just opposite the crucified Saviour, stands the Roman captain,
lifting his hand, as he gazes up at him, in the affirmation of his faith.
Especially admirable in this drawing is the quiet simplicity of the attitudes

Fig. 47. THE VIRGIN OF SOLOTHURN. Oil-painting of 1522. In a private collection at Solothurn.
(After an original photograph by Braun, Clément & Co., Dornach (Alsace) and Paris.)

and movements; where it was requisite to give an idea of lively action the artist
was capable of displaying the utmost vivacity; here, where action had come
to an end, he had the sense to avoid all forced display of energy (Fig. 33).

Fig. 48. St. Ursula. Oil-painting of 1522.
In the Kunsthalle, Carlsruhe.

The designs of Holbein for armorial windows are masterpieces of tasteful richness. Among these drawings, too, is one which can be recognised as belonging to the time of his residence at Lucerne. It is dated 1518 and displays the arms of the Lucerne family of Holdermeier. The heraldic part of the subject is limited here to the coat-of-arms, which stands on the ground; the principal subject is a group of three peasants treated in a grotesque spirit, who stand behind the shield conversing keenly; the architectural frame, an arch resting on pillars, recognisable as marble, contains in the spandrils pictures of peasants again, representing reapers and mowers (Fig. 34). When he had to design the arms of persons engaged in military pursuits the heraldic subject was naturally enriched with figures of warriors, as this drawing was with peasants; the picturesque forms of the Landsknechts in their

fantastic dress must
have appealed pe-
culiarly to Holbein's
taste. Thus, in one
drawing we find a
warrior of fierce
aspect with a strong
two-handed sword on
his shoulder em-
ployed as a suppor-
ter to the shield;
besides this the up-
per space of the
frame is adorned
with a combat of
foot-soldiers (Fig. 35).
In another very fine
drawing two lands-
knechts stand one
on either side of the
shield (Fig. 37). A
similar design with
the addition of heroic
antique figures and
of a combat of naked
men in the archi-
tectural frame, is
in the Berlin Mu-
seum (separate plate,
Fig. 36). In the two
last-named drawings
the shields are left
blank. They cannot,
therefore, have been
prepared for a de-
finite person, since
the first thing anyone
would wish would
be to see his own
armorial bearings on
the escutcheon. Hol-
bein made them,
therefore, as part of
the stock in trade of
either the glasier or

Fig. 49. St. George. Oil-painting of 1522.
In the Kunsthalle, Carlsruhe.

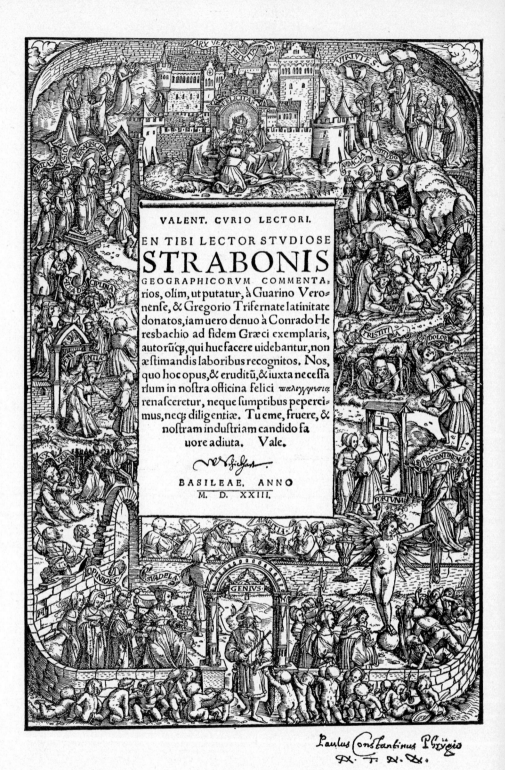

VALENT. CVRIO LECTORI.

EN TIBI LECTOR STVDIOSE
STRABONIS
GEOGRAPHICORVM COMMENTA:
rios, olim, ut putatur, à Guarino Vero‐
nense, & Gregorio Trifernate latinitate
donatos, iam uero denuo à Conrado He
resbachio ad fidem Græci exemplaris,
autorúcp, qui huc facere uidebantur, non
æstimandis laboribus recognitos. Nos,
quo hoc opus, & eruditũ, & iuxta necessa
rium in nostra officina felici παλιγγνεσια
renasceretur, neque sumptibus peperci‐
mus, necp diligentiæ. Tu eme, fruere, &
nostram industriam candido fa
uore adiuta. Vale.

BASILEAE. ANNO
M. D. XXIII.

Fig. 50. THE TABLE OF CEBES. Woodcut title-border, first published in 1522 (from a book printed in 1523, in the Royal Print Cabinet, Berlin).

himself, leaving the heraldic details to be filled in according to the requirements of the person who ordered the pattern. In another large and very handsome design for an episcopal coat-of-arms, in which the surface of the picture is almost overwrought with a too lavish abundance of forms, the shield and also the space for a motto or other inscription are left blank (Fig. 38). Two rich compositions in quite different styles contain the arms of Basle. In one of these drawings the escutcheon, supported by children, stands at the feet of the Virgin Mary; on the two

Fig. 51. ERASMUS OF ROTTERDAM. Woodcut probably cut by Hans Lützelburger.

sides stand the sainted Emperor Henry and the sainted Bishop Pantalus; the arch which encloses the design has empty shields let into the architecture, and is adorned with medallion-portraits of Roman emperors between arabesques. The other drawing, which, for a wonder, is without an architectural frame, displays the arms of Basle, with basilisks as supporters, under an arch or gateway in course of building, which again shows the circlet of blank shields; at the back we look upon a wooded landscape, and in the foreground a boat laden with soldiers passes along. The commander of the soldiers is identified by the name of Basilius, and the whole subject refers to the legendary story of the founding of Basle (Fig. 39). A design for the arms of a married couple, once more with the shields left blank, is remarkable for the spirited work of the crests on the helmets, which grow out into luxuriant ornament; for the reminiscence of the style of late Romanesque portals in the shape of the architectural frame; and for the date — 1520 — with which the drawing is signed. It appears that Holbein's heraldic drawings, as well as his other designs for glass-painting, were produced for the most part in the years which immediately followed his return from Lucerne, or at an even earlier time.

Holbein carried out one of his finest heraldic drawings, not as a pattern for stained glass, but on the wood-block. The design represents the arms of the town of Freiburg im Breisgau and adorns the title of a book which appeared in 1520, "The Municipal Laws and Statutes of the Praiseworthy Town of Freiburg". Here the heraldic design extends right across the page, leaving only a narrow space above and below for the words of the title and a few verses. The back of this title-page is also adorned with a woodcut by Holbein. It represents the patron saints of Freiburg, the Virgin Mary, the knightly St. George and the Bishop Lambert; in the architectural frame the arms of the town, a simple shield with a cross, are again introduced,

4*

Fig. 52. ERASMUS OF ROTTERDAM. Oil-painting of 1523. In the Louvre, Paris.
(After an original photograph by Braun, Clément & Co., Dornach (Alsace) and Paris.)

together with the arms of the state to which Breisgau at that time belonged,
the shield with the Austrian fesse (Fig. 40).

After Holbein had settled at Basle he had frequent opportunities offered
to him of displaying the art of which he had given proof at Lucerne, by
embellishing the street-front of houses with decorative paintings. Of these
street-paintings nothing has been preserved. There are only a few original
designs for single pieces (Fig. 41) and, occasionally, later copies, to give us
an idea of their style. With bold fancy and ingenious turning to account
of the different kinds of space produced by the irregular placing of the
windows, he clothed the plain houses with Renaissance architecture rich in
columns and enlivened the painted balconies and airy porticoes with historical
or mythological figures, symbols, or popular types. Most famous of all was
the painting of peasants dancing in wild merriment, from which the house
on which it was done derived the name of "the Dance-House". Besides

the original designs for single parts which are extant, there is an old tracing of the general design, which preserves a record of the appearance of the building when thus painted. It was a corner-house in three storeys; the painting was spread over both sides, and the perspective was so calculated that it reckoned on the spectator standing at an angle opposite to the corner of the building, from which he would see both sides at once. On the ground-floor, on the principal side, there was a painted arcade resting on pillars; Holbein had very cleverly made use of the Gothic forms of door and windows, as they actually existed, in such a way that the pointed arches, which did not suit his style, appeared to be the result of the diminution

Fig. 53. THE CONSORT OF DUKE JOHN OF BERRY.
Drawing in black and coloured chalk from the painted stone figure of the duchess in the Cathedral at Bourges. In the Basle Museum.
(After an original photograph by Braun, Clément & Co., Dornach (Alsace) and Paris.)

in perspective of the round arches painted on the wall, as seen in the slanting view incidental to the spectator's standpoint. Over that, in the space beneath the next row of windows, appeared the coloured figures of the dancing peasants at their revels on a boarded floor, casting their shadows aslant on the wall, where the architecture appeared to recede further to make room for them. On the other side of the house a large part of the wall was painted to give the effect of a view into a lofty doorway which cut into the first storey as well. On the farther side of this there was again a painted arcade; in front of it was seen a groom, standing with a horse; since it was not appropriate to paint them as if standing in the street, their feet were concealed by a low wall which was supposed to run along the side of the street. Further up, between the windows of the first storey, there was a figure of Bacchus in colours. The upper floors on both walls of the

house were covered with intricate and fantastic architecture. Now seeming
to project in balconies on which gay figures were moving, now retreating
to a distance, interrupted by vistas ending in blue sky under shady arches,
decorated with stone figures and medallions, this piece of artistic jesting
displayed an abundance of the most varied motives. Even the irregularities
produced by the position of the windows were turned to account, for the
artist made it appear as if the inequalities were occasioned by the perspective.
Over the painted doorway one perceived Marcus Curtius, who sprang forward
from a deep portico and was on the point of leaping down into the street
with his great white horse rearing up. The painter did not omit to put in
a little joke of his own; quite at the top there stood on a cornice a
paint-pot, as if it had been forgotten there and could not now be fetched
down. A realism which went so far as to deceive the eye was a favourite
piece of wit in Holbein's street-paintings. There are several tales bearing
on this point which the authors of the old narratives thought worth recording.
The town of Basle had so many house-fronts painted by Holbein that it
must really have borne the impress of his personal style. But the influence
of the young painter with his cultivated taste was not confined to the decoration of houses; it extended even to the outward appearance of the people.
Among the drawings by Holbein in the Basle Museum are a number of
designs for ladies' costumes. It can hardly be supposed that Holbein would
have made these carefully washed drawings on a fairly large scale merely in
order to inform posterity how the women of Basle were dressed in his day;
he rather applied his gift of invention, which amused itself with producing
new varieties of form in structure and ornament within the "antique" style
which was driving out the Gothic, to another purpose — that of creating
patterns of feminine costume on the lines of the prevailing fashion. And
there can be no doubt that those young ladies who let their dressmakers translate these patterns into actual costumes looked very well in them. The
dresses offer a great deal of variety. Here we see a lady of good position
in a dress of rich and heavy silk with wide, puffed sleeves, under which
appear the lower sleeves in several puffs of fine white material, with a
broad hat trimmed all round with waving ostrich-plumes (Fig. 42). Then
a lady in a gala-dress for the house, a cloth gown with wide velvet trimming, ornamented with various puffs and pleats of white material on the
breast and arms, with embroidered petticoat and embroidered cap, and a
quantity of gold ornaments over the transparent stuff which forms a light
veil over the shoulders (Fig. 43). Further on is the very pretty drawing
of a citizen's wife in a pleated gown and transparent cap. Then the so-
called hostess, a young lady who is represented with a bumper in her hand,
as if just discharging the duty of pledging a guest; to correspond with
this she wears the domestic apron, which with its delicate folds is in itself a
piece of finery, over the richly pleated gown with a train and sleeves divided
into several wide pleated puffs; on her head she wears a perfectly flat
hat placed on one side, the rim of which is surrounded by a circle of

Fig. 54. THE PASSION OF CHRIST IN EIGHT PICTURES.
Altar-piece (general view, cf. the two following double illustrations). In the Basle Museum.
(After an original photograph by Braun, Clément & Co., Dornach (Alsace) and Paris.)

ostrich-feathers and she has almost disguised the cut of the bodice under a velvet-trimmed collar which comes down to her shoulders, and is not unlike the modern cape. The finest of all these drawings from the artistic point of view is that of a citizen's wife seen half from the back, in a comparatively simple but, nevertheless, becoming costume; the one ornament of the gown of heavy cloth consists of a velvet trimming to the bodice and to the smooth sleeves, which are interrupted only at the elbows by puffs of white material; on the neck and shoulders there rests a thin material in folds, and the hair is hidden under a half-transparent cap; there is no ornament of metal, only the artfully wrought case for sewing requisites which hangs on the girdle (Fig. 44). As regards the sixth of these drawings of the fashions, showing a young girl of rather jaunty appearance in a hat and feathers, with her dress cut very low and unveiled, the attribution to Holbein

Fig. 55. LOWER HALF OF TI

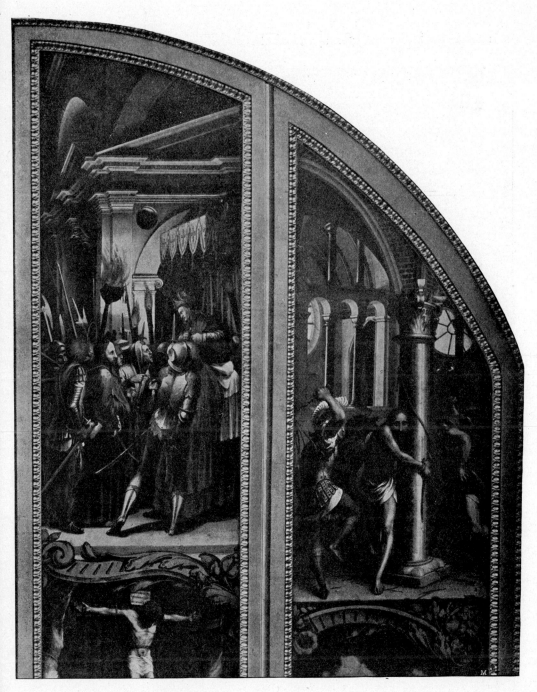

PAINTING OF THE PASSION in the Basle Museum.
　　　　　(After an original photograph by Braun, Clément & Co., Dornach (Alsace) and Paris.)

appears doubtful. What strikes the modern spectator as so odd in all these picture of feminine costume, the backward bend of the body and the hollow back, was a fashionable habit of the time, quite a part of good manners, which arose perhaps from the circumstance, that the occasionally

Fig. 56. LOWER HALF OF THE PAINTING

very heavy dress came just as far down to the ground in front as it did behind, and had to be constantly lifted up in front in walking.

It was to the young painter, of whose taste and inventive talent Basle beheld so many proofs and whose manual dexterity in wall-painting was displayed on the houses along the streets, that the government of Basle applied when the question arose of decorating the interior of the great council-chamber in the new town-hall with frescoes. Holbein undertook this task in June 1521 and brought it to a provisional conclusion by the late autumn of the following year. In this time he painted three walls of the chamber. When he had finished them he considered that he had already earned the price agreed upon for the whole; the council recognised his claim

OF THE PASSION in the Basle Museum.
(After an original photograph by Braun, Clément & Co., Dornach (Alsace) and Paris.)

and resolved "to let the back wall alone till further orders". What a magnificent work Holbein produced here, we can, unfortunately, only guess from such means as we have of becoming acquainted with it. The paintings themselves have long since perished, probably owing to damp. Traces of them were discovered in the year 1817, in removing some old tapestry. After this copies were made of three of the principal subjects, which, of course, reproduce no more than the general idea of the composition. We get a better notion of the actual forms which occurred in the paintings from a washed drawing by Holbein, which has served as a design for one of the pictures, and from several old copies of similar designs. How splendid the colour must have been we can only guess from a few sorry fragments which have been detached from the crumbling plaster of the walls and placed in the Museum. In decorating the hall the artist proceeded on the same principles which he applied in painting the exterior of houses. He transformed what in itself was a simple room into a wide hall by painting rows of columns. Within this general frame he arranged the figure-subjects in such a way that the actions depicted in the principal paintings took place in wide vistas seen through the architecture, as if outside, now in the open air, now in deep porticoes; in the intervals between these large pictures one saw single figures in recessed niches let into the frame of the architecture. These single figures were partly historical characters, partly allegories of the so-called profane, or cardinal virtues. For the principal pictures the material was derived from ancient history, as the fashion of the day required; they were designed to encourage, by magnificent examples, the most rigorous exercise of those virtues which are the highest duties of the ruler. Inflexible justice and self-sacrificing constancy were personified in the pictures of two lawgivers: Charondas, who condemned himself to the penalty of death, and Zaleucus, who paid in his own person half of the penalty which his son had incurred; an example of wisdom was given in the picture of the incorruptible Dentatus, and moderation was preached by the deterrent example of the Persian king Sapor, who inflicted further humiliation on his vanquished foe. Even the imperfect means of study which the extant sketches and the bad copies afford, enable us to realise in how telling and lively a manner Holbein narrated these events.

Charondas of Catanea, in the laws which he gave to the town of Thurii, had on pain of death forbidden the wearing of arms in the assembly of the people; it occurred one day that he returned from a journey, hurried to the assembly without changing his attire and did not perceive till he was there that he was still girt with his sword; thereupon he put himself to death before the eyes of all. Holbein has placed the sitting of the representatives of the people of Thurii in a large hall with columns, partly open, richly adorned with sculpture. The eyes of all in the assembly are fixed on Charondas, and the latter carries out his astonishing action so rapidly that most of them remain seated in their places as if spellbound; only a few have jumped up. Charondas lifts his eyes to heaven as he buries the sword in his breast, according to the purport of the old narrative: that his last words were an invocation to Zeus to bear witness that law must still reign supreme.

The picture of Zaleucus represent with a ruthless realism the blinding of two men. In a hall which opens upon a sunlit square there sits before a great crowd of spectators a young man whose left eye is being plucked out by the gaoler. Opposite to him sits a dignified old man in princely

garb on a throne, offering his right eye to the pincers. The old man is
Zaleucus, ruler of Locri in the South of Italy. His laws had punished
adultery by the loss of both eyes, and his only son had been convicted of
this crime. The Locrians begged him to grant mercy; and in order to

Fig. 57. "Touch me not!" (Joh. XX. 17). Oil-painting in the picture-gallery at Hampton Court. From the first annual series of the Society for photographical publications illustrating the history of art.

yield to their entreaties and to his own paternal feelings without a deviation
from the law, he decided that his son was to lose one eye, whilst he himself
would sacrifice the other. It is wonderful how the artist has depicted the
contrast between the culprit, who endures his punishment in fearful torment,
and the hero of self-sacrifice, who makes ready to suffer the same penalty

of his own accord. On the one the minister of justice discharges his duty without compunction. In the other case the man charged to execute the order first examines the eye with a lens; we see that he will take pains to proceed with the operation as carefully as possible. The people are partly looking with deep emotion at the prince, and partly watching, horror-struck, the gaoler's work.

The sheet in the Basle Museum which contains the old copy sketched from the painting of Zaleucus shows us also one of the allegorical figures which Holbein arranged between the historical pictures. It is the figure of Justice. Dame Justice stands in an architectural arcade and points with her sword to a tablet hung upon the arch, on which are the words

Fig. 58. THE NATIVITY. Wing of an altar-piece in the Minster at Freiburg.
(After an original photograph published by G. Röbke, Freiburg.)

in the Latin language: "O, ye rulers, forget
your own affairs and be careful for
those of the public". The other
subjects, too, were explained
by inscriptions.

Of the picture of
Curius Dentatus no
sketch, unfortuna-
tely, is extant, but
only the defec-
tive copy of
the remnants
discovered in
1817. The
picture must
have been
splendid; the
composition
is very fine.

Under an
open portico
of round ar-
ches, through
which there
is a wide view
of a lands-
cape, Curius,
clad in the
armour of a
Roman gene-
ral, kneels by
the fire on
the hearth
and is in the
act of pre-
paring his
simple meal
with his own
hands. There
enter from
one side the
envoys of the
Samnites; the
two foremost
of the sump-

Fig. 59. THE ADORATION OF THE MAGI. Wing of an altar-piece in the Minster at Freiburg
After an original photograph published by G. Röbke, Freiburg.)

Fig. 60. THE MAN OF SORROWS. Oil-painting in shades of brown. In the Basle Museum.
(After an original photograph by Braun, Clément & Co., Dornach (Alsace) and Paris.)

Fig. 61. MATER DOLOROSA. Oil-painting in shades of brown. In the Basle Museum.
(After an original photograph by Braun, Clément & Co, Dornach (Alsace) and Paris.)

KNACKFUSS, Hans Holbein.

5

Fig. 62. Design for the left wing of the organ-case in the Minster at Basle.
Drawing washed with brown, in the Basle Museum.
(After an original photograph by Braun, Clément & Co., Dornach (Alsace)
and Paris.)

tuously attired lords, in Renaissance costume, carry a great golden goblet and a bowl full of gold pieces. The Roman, however, merely turns round a little way towards them, and says, as he points to the turnips in front of him, the words which are written on the picture: "I prefer to eat these off my earthenware and rule over those who have gold". Under this subject the painter has filled up the remaining space of the wall in a peculiar way. We see the stone vault underneath the pavement on which the action takes place; in front of the vaulted cellar stands the messenger of the Basle town-council, arrayed in the armorial colours of the town (black and white) with the coat-of-arms upon his breast, who doffs his hat in salutation to the spectator. Of the original painting the heads of some of the envoys are preserved; in spite of their damaged condition we can still admire the excellence of the painting on them.

Of the picture of Sapor the design by Holbein's own hand is extant, a washed drawing to which a more lively and picturesque effect is given by a few touches of colour laid on here and there. The architectural frame which encloses the subject shows richly decorated columns on red marble bases. Between them there is a view of an open square, ending in late-Gothic buildings. Knights and armed men on foot fill the square. In the foreground the Persian king Sapor, in stately Renaissance attire, mounts his horse, which is held by a groom, while he uses the back of the captive Emperor Valerian, who kneels on the ground with a scornful expression, as his footstool.

In the two years during which Holbein was painting in the Town-hall, he produced various oil paintings, which are preserved to posterity. A remarkable picture in the Basle Museum which irresistibly rivets the gaze of the spectator, Christ in the tomb (Fig. 45—46), is dated 1521. The corpse lies outstretched in the narrow coffin, of which the side directed towards us is omitted in the painting, with nothing laid under it but a white sheet upon the ground. The interior of the coffin is painted a warm green and

Fig. 63. DESIGN FOR THE RIGHT WING OF THE ORGAN-CASE IN THE MINSTER AT BASLE.
Drawing washed with brown, in the Basle Museum.
(After an original photograph by Braun, Clément & Co., Dornach (Alsace) and Paris.)

this tone suits the pale grey tones of the dead body wonderfully. Over the cover of the coffin there is a narrow strip of deep-black background to be seen, and over that is the inscription "Jesus Nazarenus Rex Judaeorum", as if written in letters of gold on the edge of a slab of white stone. Holbein painted the corpse from nature with the utmost pains; he has rendered the rigidity of the limbs, the lifelessness of the skin, the colourless face with the bloodless lips, and the sunken eyes with perfect accuracy. His model was certainly not beautiful, but there is an unspeakable beauty in the picture, though not, indeed, in the current sense of the word. It is a marvel of painting. It is true that the picture receives its religious significance only from the stigmata and from the superscription; there is no question of ideal conception; it was clearly just the painter's business to make the most of an opportunity for study which did not often come in his way. Basilius Amerbach himself quoted the picture very appositely in his catalogue as "a picture of a dead man, with the title Jesus of Nazareth".

5 *

Fig. 64. VIRGIN AND CHILD. Pen-drawing, washed and heightened with
white on paper with a grey ground. In the Basle Museum.
(After an original photograph by Braun, Clément & Co., Dornach (Alsace)
and Paris.)

The date 1522 is on a picture now in a private collection at Solothurn, which is known as the "Madonna of Solothurn" (Fig. 47). It, doubtless, originally adorned an altar in the old minster of that town, which minster was replaced by a new building in the last century. It was found at a later time, uncared for and injured by neglect, in the church of a neighbouring village. It represents, with a composition greatly resembling that of the woodcut with the patron-saints of Freiburg (Fig. 40), the Virgin Mary enthroned between the standing figures of a bishop and a knight; these two are the patron-saints of Solothurn, St. Martin, Bishop of Tours, and St. Ursus, one of the martyrs of the Theban Legion. The head of the Virgin is the most gracious and lovely feminine head which Holbein ever designed. Looking to the front with an expression of modesty and affability, the Virgin holds the naked child, delightfully true to life, moving its head and little hands and feet, upon her lap. Over her light-red dress the blue mantle falls in wide folds down to the steps of the throne, which are covered with a bright carpet, ornamented with the arms of the donors. The head, with the golden hair spread over the shoulders, on which there lies a fine, transparent veil, and the rich crown set with precious stones and pearls, stand out against the light-blue of the sky, of which there is a view through a round arch. This grey stone arch, contrary to Holbein's custom, is quite without ornament; iron rods are stretched across and fixed in it, as if to kee pit together. This expedient had probably been tried to strengthen the vaulting of the old church, and Holbein brought the picture into harmony with the architecture under which it was placed. The two saints at the sides are splendid figures; admirable, too, is the way in which

Fig. 65. HOLY FAMILY. Washed drawing, heightened with white, on paper with a red ground.
In the Basle Museum
(After an original photograph by Braun, Clément & Co., Dornach (Alsace) and Paris.)

Fig. 66. CHRIST FALLING UNDER THE WEIGHT OF THE CROSS.
Washed drawing, heightened with white, on a grey ground. In the Basle Museum.
(After an original photograph by Braun, Clément & Co., Dornach (Alsace) and Paris.)

the contrast of character is brought out; St. Martin is a well-bred man and
a good priest, with a refined, intelligent and amiable face; his red mitre
and violet chasuble are decorated with splendid embroidery, which the
painter has carried out in the most minute detail; in his left hand he holds,
together with his pastoral staff, the glove stripped from his right hand,
which he uses to put some pieces of money into a beggar's wooden bowl.
The beggar is introduced as one of the attributes which characterize St. Martin;
Holbein has had the good sense to let no more than is necessary appear
of this figure, which in itself is not appropriate to the gathering of saints;
he shows the miserable, imploring face and a bit of the hand which holds
up the bowl to receive the gift. St. Ursus is quite the warrior, faultless
and inflexible; clad from head to foot in the armour which was worn in
the artist's own time, he grasps the hilt of his sword in his left hand, and
holds in his right hand a red flag with a white cross, which is reflected in
the shining steel of helmet and cuirass.

Two panels with single figures of saints, now in the gallery at Carlsruhe (evidently parts of a larger altar-piece) belong also to the year 1522.
One picture, in which the date is introduced together with the artist's name,
represents St. Ursula. Crowned with a golden nimbus, in princely costume
according to the taste of the time, the witness to the faith stands in front
of a wide landscape and blue sky, which is intersected by the branches of

a fig-tree; she holds a number of long arrows in her hands as the token of her martyrdom (Fig. 48). The companion-picture represents St. George in antique armour, standing, flag in hand, upon the prostrate dragon (Fig. 49).

In the same year appeared for the first time a famous woodcut title-border by Holbein, which was often reprinted, the Table of Cebes, as it is called. The Greek philosopher Cebes — either the pupil of Socrates mentioned by Plato, or a later person of the same name — describes in detail in his writing, "The Picture", a painting of many figures which was shown to him in a temple; it represented the progress of man to true happiness. From this description Holbein designed the above-mentioned title-page (Fig. 50). A wall running round the picture betokens the limited space of human life. Outside the wall, at the lower edge of the picture, we see a group of naked children. These are the souls of men who have not entered upon life; the form of a child was universally recognised in the Middle Ages as a symbol of the soul, and was still a current mode of representing it in Holbein's time. The soul on entering life is received at the portal by the Genius, or protecting spirit, represented as a dignified old man, who offers a scroll as each enters; the contents of the scroll are, presumably, the admonitions of the guardian-spirit for the path of life. Immediately behind the portal of life the Goddess of Fortune passes by on a rolling sphere, dealing out good and evil, and Persuasion, symbolized by a woman richly dressed, waits for the novice in life, with a ministering train of misleading Opinions. What enticements they offer, the wayfarer, who now appears in the form of a young man, can see on the other side of a wall. The gate in this wall leads him into the region of Lust, of Avarice, and of Incontinence. After he has passed through the gate which leads out of this domain, Pain and Sorrow wait for him by the way. From their domain he is conducted by Penitence, who takes him lovingly by the

Fig. 67. CHRIST BEARING THE CROSS. Woodcut (unique impression) in the Basle Museum.

Fig. 68. Nude figure of uncertain meaning.
Washed drawing, heightened with white, on reddish paper. In the Basle Museum.
(After an original photograph by Braun, Clément & Co., Dornach (Alsace) and Paris.)

hand. But now he falls a victim to False Doctrine, who appears as another lady in fine clothes. Only a narrow path and a strait gate in the
precipitous cliff lead out of this region; the crowd of people who think
that thay have found the goal of life are encamped here, against the rock,
keenly bent on various occupations. The wanderer through life looks at
the beautiful woman in timid admiration — this little expressive figure,
drawn from the back, is really a masterpiece — and passes on. In Daring
and Fortitude he finds the auxiliary powers which pull him through the

narrow, rocky pass, in which the pathway disappears. And now he has
arrived at the region of True Doctrine. She stands in form like the image
of a saint upon a stone base; Truth and Conviction are her attendants. The
traveller through life kneels down before her in veneration and now nothing
hinders him from entrance to the citadel of True Happiness. There
dwell all the Virtues, and in the centre Happiness sits on her throne, a
princess encircled by a halo of supernatural beams; she crowns the traveller, who has turned aside from every path of error and found the true
way. Holbein seldom signed his drawings on wood with his name, but he
thought this design sufficiently important to place his signature 'on it, in
the form of a double H.

Holbein's Table of Cebes was originally destined to adorn the title of
the Latin edition of the New Testament brought out by Erasmus of Rotterdam. That explains the ecclesiastical shape given to the figures of True
Doctrine and of Happiness. The application of the idea of the Greek
philosopher to the Christian book was quite after the mind of Erasmus.

In the same year, 1522, there appeared at Basle a German edition of
the New Testament, a reprint of Luther's translation, and for this book, too,
Holbein designed the title. He introduced, as principal figures at the sides,
the Apostles Peter and Paul, in the four corners the symbols of the Evangelists, above the arms of the town of Basle and below the printer's mark
of the publisher, Adam Petri, a child riding on a lion.

In march, 1523, Petri published, together with a new issue of this large
edition, a small octavo edition, beautifully got up, of the New Testament

Fig. 69. FIGHT OF LANDSKNECHTS. Washed drawing in the Basle Museum.
(After an original photograph by Braun, Clément & Co., Dornach (Alsace) and Paris.

in the German translation. This was adorned with a title of similar composition to the large one already described, and also with the figures of
the four Evangelists and with four subjects from the Acts of the Apostles
by Holbein's hand.

In December, 1523, Petri published a reprint of Luther's translation
of the Old Testament. This book contained, in addition to many little cuts
by other draughtsmen, a number of ornamental initials and some cuts by
Holbein, among them being a particularly fine heading at the beginning of the

Fig. 70. A SHIP PREPARED TO SAIL, WITH ARMED MEN ON BOARD. Washed drawing in the Städel Institute,
Frankfort on the Maine.

text, representing the creation of Eve in the midst of the other already
accomplished works of the Creator. A larger series of drawings on wood
by Holbein was designed for the edition of Luther's translation of the New
Testament, which the printer Thomas Wolff brought out — also in the year
1523. Here he arranged a number of subjects together as a title-border,
taken chiefly from the Acts of the Apostles. He added twenty-one illustrations to the Revelations of St. John. It is no reproach to Holbein if in
spite of his usual independence as an artist, he was not always successful on
this occasion, in keeping free from reminiscences of the powerful creations
of Dürer; and it will be readily understood that he did not succeed in
reaching the level of his great predecessor, especially in respect of imagi-

Fig. 71. THE ALPHABET OF THE DANCE OF DEATH.
Designs cut on the wood by Hans Lützelburger (Same size as the original).

Fig. 72. DEATH AND THE EMPEROR. From the woodcut series of the Dance of Death. (Same size as the original.)

nation. The woodcuts to the Apocalypse were badly engraved. The title-page, on the other hand, with its multitude of small figures, is a master-piece of the wood-engraver's art. It bears the mark of the wood-engraver, Hans Lützelburger.

Hans Lützelburger, called Franck, most likely came from Augsburg. He appears not to have come to Basle till 1523. His period of activity there lasted only a few years; he was already dead in June 1526. But during this time he cut almost all Holbein's designs for printed books. He had a masterly skill in most exactly reproducing the artist's line, especially in little, delicate things. It is only in the illustrations which were cut by him that the beauty of Holbein's drawing on wood can be properly appreciated.

He is, no doubt, responsible for the marvellously distinct cutting of the little portrait of Erasmus of Rotterdam, which Holbein drew for the publisher Froben (Fig. 51). This little round portrait, which sets before our eyes the sharp profile and delicate features of the prematurely old scholar with such a life-like distinctness that the little drawing takes rank with large paintings, must have been produced in the year 1523.

In this year Erasmus had his portrait taken by Holbein several times. In a letter to Willibald Pirkheimer at Nuremberg Erasmus mentions these portraits, which he had sent to friends abroad, two to England and one to France. The two portraits which were sent to England are still extant. One is in an English private collection. The other went to Paris as a present from King Charles I. of England to Louis XIII., and is now in the Louvre. This is a master-piece of the first rank. Erasmus is represented writing — two-thirds of the size of life. He has just written the heading of a new work on a sheet of paper, which lies before him supported on a book; his eyes follow the movement of the classical implement of writing, the reed-pen, which he uses instead of a quill. Every feature in face and hands is perfectly true to life. The skin is colourless, the hair turning grey. The costume is dark — black prevailing.

Fig. 73. DEATH AND THE SAILOR. From the woodcut series, the Dance of Death.

The background is a dark-green tapestry with a pattern in light-green and white, and a piece of brown panelling at the side. The harmony of colour is the most perfect imaginable (Fig. 52).

The Museum at Basle possesses the study for the last-named portrait of Erasmus, which was painted in oils on paper and subsequently fastened down on a panel. This preliminary study is a finished picture in itself. It is distinguished from the Paris portrait, apart from the less finished execution of the painting, only by the plain background and a few differences in the costume, which are not so advantageous for the picturesque effect of the whole. It has been suggested, not without good rea-

Fig. 74. DEATH AND THE KNIGHT.
From the woodcut series, the Dance of Death.

sons, that the Basle portrait is the one which Erasmus sent to France, according to the already mentioned letter, and that its recipient was Bonifacius Amerbach. Bonifacius was then staying, for the purpose of renewing his studies, at Avignon, and the Basle portrait of Erasmus writing comes from his collection. In the letter it is stated that Erasmus had his portrait conveyed to France by the painter himself. This circumstance, too, confirms the correctness of the conjecture, since Holbein, like Erasmus, was a personal friend of Amerbach.

It seems that Holbein made use of this occasion for a lengthy journey through France. Two drawings in the Basle Museum tell of a visit of the artist to Bourges. These drawings represent a gentleman and lady in the costume of the first quarter of the 15th century, kneeling in prayer. They are copies of the effigies of the Duke Jehan de Berry (dated 1416) and his consort, in the Cathedral at Bourges (in Holbein's time they were still in the private chapel of the Dukes of Berry) when this chapel was pulled down they were placed in the ambulatory of the choir. Holbein has copied these sepulchral effigies, of which the lady's more especially is very pleasing and full of expression (Fig. 53), just as if he were drawing from life, and has introduced quite a lively and picturesque effect into the drawing in black chalk by a few touches of colour in red and yellow crayons.

A fourth likeness of Erasmus, which

Fig. 75. DEATH AND THE MARRIED COUPLE.
From the woodcut series, the Dance of Death.

Fig. 76. DEATH AND THE PLOUGHMAN.
From the woodcut series, the Dance of Death.

Holbein painted about the same time, was the half of a double picture representing the learned author and his meritorious publisher, Froben. It was ordered by Erasmus as a present for the latter. This picture has been lost sight of. A copy of the whole is in England, and a copy of the bust of Froben alone is in the Museum at Basle. The latter copy is very bad as regards colouring. But it is at any rate interesting to become acquainted through it with the appearance of the man who gave Holbein the opportunity of producing so many of his works. Johannes Froben, who sits with his arms crossed in a black over-coat lined with brown fur, shows us a clean-shaven, wrinkled face, the features of which are rather common, though it has a striking expression of benevolence and cleverness; the scanty brown hair, of moderate length, falls down the back of the head.

The years 1524 and 1525 are not to be found on any extant work of Holbein. So several undated pictures may be mentioned here, which may have been produced about this time.

For centuries it was thought that Holbein's crowning effort was a series of eight small pictures of the Passion of Christ arranged in one frame (Fig. 54, 55, 56). This painting had been kept from time immemorial in the town-hall at Basle. But as it was painted, in all probability, not for the town-hall itself but for a church, it is supposed that the town-council took possession of it to protect it from damage or destruction in the iconoclastic distur-bances which Basle went through in 1529. Maximilian I., Elector of Bavaria, the zealous collector who obtained Dürer's Apostles by purchase from the town of Nuremberg, was anxious to become pos-sessed of this Passion at any price. But the people of Basle showed more esteem for the memory of their great artist than Nuremberg did for the legacy of Dürer, and dismissed the Elector's envoys with a courteous but emphatic refusal. The pic-ture remained in the possession of the town, and told everyone who visited the town-hall of the fame and honour of the

Fig. 77. DEATH AND THE GAMBLERS.
From the woodcut series, the Dance of Death.

master. Joachim von Sandrart speaks of it in his "Teutsche Akademie" (1675) as "a work in which everything may be found of which our art is capable", and one which need not "yield the palm to any picture either in Germany or in Italy". This lasted till the year 1771. The picture was then ceded by a resolution of the council to the collection of art which now occupies the Museum. On this occasion it had the misfortune, before it was transferred, to be submitted to a "thorough restoration", in which it was robbed of the best part of its beauty. The painter who restored it, treated the drawing, it is true, with praiseworthy consideration, but he destroyed the colour. In the work of renovation he certainly painted what was

Fig. 78. THE ARMS OF DEATH.
From the woodcut series, the Dance of Death.

red, red, and what was blue, blue, and so forth, but he spoilt the harmony of the tones and also annihilated by his smooth finish the delicate charm of Holbein's brush-work. Through the hard and gaudy discords of the colouring the charm of Holbein's harmony can no longer be perceived. Anyone with a susceptible eye for beauty has to get over the annoyance caused by this lifeless colouring before he can succeed in enjoying the great beauties which the picture otherwise possesses. What will strike him first is the admirable manner in which the eight separate paintings, standing in two rows, one above the other, divided horizontally by painted ornaments of gold, vertically by the bars of a frame standing out in relief, are combined into a single picturesque composition. Each of the eight subjects (which are adapted very cleverly to the tall shape of the separate compartments) is a picture complete in itself, possessing its definite, picturesque effects of light and shade, which might stand quite on its own merits as a work of art. But, at the same time, the whole produces the effect of a single painting: the lights and shadows are so distributed that the whole picture, too, presents itself to the eye as a single and complete work of art. Every composition taken separately is a master-piece of life and expression. The various ways in which the light is managed help to produce a

Fig. 79. THE LAST JUDGMENT.
From the woodcut series, the Dance of Death.

Fig. 80. Isaac blessing Jacob (Gen. XXVII. 23).
From the woodcut to the Old Testament (same size as the original).

telling and vivid effect. In the first of the small pictures, Christ praying on the Mount of Olives, the angel with the chalice appears in a radiant break in the darkness of the sky. In the two following, Christ taken captive and Christ led before the High-Priest, the illumination proceeds from torches; in the former the torch-light plays on the lower boughs of a tree, the top of which is lost in darkness; in the latter it flickers among the fantastic shapes of one of Holbein's Renaissance buildings. In the fourth and fifth pictures, too, the Scourging and Mocking of Christ, the figures are surrounded by rich fancy architecture. In the next two subjects, Christ bearing the Cross and the Crucifixion, the lower halves of the pictures are quite filled by the figures; over these appear, in the first, a round tower over a gate in the town-wall and an extensive landscape in bright daylight with a range of mountains in the distance; while, in the second, where the cross is erected, the sky behind it is as black as pitch. The Entombment is the last of the series; men are carrying the sacred body across a green meadow to the entrance of the tomb, hewn in a yellow rock; the Virgin stands weeping, with her attendants round her, near a fig-tree which has taken root in a cleft of the rock.

Closely allied to these pictures of the Passion, both in sentiment and in the way in which the subject has presented itself for treatment to the painter, is a small picture which has been recently discovered, so

Fig. 81. Boaz and Ruth (Ruth II. 5).
From the woodcut to the Old Testament.

to speak, in the collection at Hampton Court near London. Its subject is also taken from the story of Christ's Passion:

Christ appearing after the Resurrection to St. Mary Magdalen (Fig. 57). It is a wonderful master-piece of poetical painting. The landscape admirably suggests "the early morning, when it was yet dark". No

Fig. 82. HANNAH SORROWING (I. Samuel I. 15).
From the woodcut to the Old Testament.

less admirable and striking is the expression of the figures. "She turned herself, and saith unto him, Rabboni. Jesus saith unto her, Touch me not." On one side we see the stone which was rolled away from the sepulchre, and through the low opening of the grave we perceive what Mary Magdalen had seen when she stooped and looked in, the two angels in white raiment, one at the head and one at the foot. In the distance the two disciples who had been before her at the sepulchre are on their way home; in the way in which they are speaking one to another the difference of the impression which the condition of the tomb has made upon each is markedly characterised, in close adherence to the text of the narrative in the Gospel of St. John, like everything else in this picture: John "saw and believed", Peter is not yet convinced of the fact of the Resurrection, and that is the reason why he speaks so eagerly.

To this group of religious pictures composed with a rich, picturesque effect of light and shade belong, further, two wings of an altar in the Minster at Freiburg im Breisgau. From the arms of

Fig. 83. SOLOMON BLESSING THE CONGREGATION (II. Chron. VI. 3).
From the woodcut to the Old Testament.

Fig. 84. The return from the Babylonian Captivity (I. Ezra I. 5).
From the woodcut to the Old Testament.

the families of Ober-
riedt and Zschecka-
pürlin, which are in-
troduced along with
the portraits of the
donor's family under
the actual subject,
we learn that Hol-
bein painted these
pictures by order
of the Basle coun-
cillor Hans Ober-
riedt, who had mar-
ried one of the
Zscheckapürlin fa-
mily. From the
shape of the pictures
it is evident that they were placed on either side of a central picture, arched at
the top, which could be closed with the aid of these wings. No doubt the
whole work was an offering from the person who gave the order to some
church at Basle. Hans Oberriedt left his native town in consequence of the
furious religious strife of the year 1529, and settled at Freiburg im Breisgau.
It was probably he who rescued the wings before the outbreak of iconoclasm
to which the larger middle panel must have fallen a victim, in order to
take them with him to his new home, and there set them up once more
over an altar. But, even so, the pictures did not obtain a permanent resting-
place. During the Thirty Years War they were sent for safety to Schaff-
hausen. The Elector Maximilian I. of Bavaria had them brought to Munich
for his inspection, and the Emperor Ferdinand III. had them shown to him
at Regensburg. In the year 1798 they were taken away from Freiburg by
the French, but were returned in 1808. Then they were placed over the
altar of the University Chapel in the choir of the Minster of Freiburg. These
are the only two church-pictures by Holbein which still confront the spectator
in a consecrated place. And, for all that, there is perhaps less religious
feeling in them than in the rest; the artist has surrendered himself more
to the purely picturesque charm than to the emotional interest of the figures.
The subjects of the two paintings, in which the figures are on a very small
scale, as in the pictures of the Passion, are the Nativity of Christ and the
Adoration of the Three Wise Men from the East. The Nativity (Fig. 58)
takes place in the ruins of a splendid ancient building. The illumination
proceeds from the little child, which is laid in white swaddling-clothes on its
bed. The supernatural light beams with a soft brilliance over the figures
of Mary and Joseph, who bend over the child in admiration and joyous
devotion, and over a group of little angels who surround him with rejoicings.
It touches up the face and shoulders of a shepherd, who stays in shy retreat

behind a pillar, wait-
ing for the arrival of
his companions, to
whom, in the distan-
ce, the radiant form
of an angel is bring-
ing the glad tidings.
The light beams
with undiminished
power beyond the
immediate surroun-
dings of the child; it
disperses the dark-
ness and allows se-
veral portions of
the marble building
to emerge with their

Fig. 85. THE PROPHET AMOS (Amos I. 1).
From the woodcut to the Old Testament.

varied shapes and colours. The moon stands in the sky. But it does
not suffer its beams to come into conflict with the sacred light. The
moon, too, by bending before him, does homage to the Lord of the
whole earth, who is born as a child: the disc of the moon — the moon
being, of course, imagined as a disc and not as a sphere — turns its
surface down towards the child, so that it appears to the spectator to
be foreshortened. Another original idea of the artist is, that in the little
angels he makes the connection of the wings with the human form
more natural, by letting the pinions develop from the arms, instead of
issuing, as they usually do, from the shoulders, as independent limbs. In
the other painting (Fig. 59), the star which had led the three wise men
forms a counterpart to the moon of the Christmas night; it stands large
and with golden beams among white clouds in the bright noonday sky. One
of the attendants of the strangers holds his hand over his eyes, to look up
towards its radiance. The scene of the event is again an antique ruin, but
seen here from the outside and plainer in its forms. A splendidly picturesque
figure is that of the Moorish king, clad in white, who waits, as the youngest
of the three, till the others have presented their gifts. The eldest, an old
man with a long beard in a red coat and ermine collar — his figure is drawn
with a singular lack of grace — offers his present on his knees to the child
seated on Mary's lap, who looks down attentively. The second of the three
wise men, a dark-bearded, powerful man, who bears a white riband with
fluttering ends twined about his crown, is preparing to step forward to take
the place of the old man as soon as he stands up. It seems that this
picture is more seriously injured by repairs than the other.

Whilst in the pictures just mentioned Holbein worked with rich colours
and full contrasts of light and shade, he contented himself in other cases
with carrying out his designs in a single colour, or hardly more, in order

Fig. 86. JAKOB MEYER. Drawing in black and coloured chalk, study for the picture of the Madonna at Darmstadt. In the Basle Museum.
(After an original photograph by Braun, Clément & Co., Dornach (Alsace) and Paris.)

to attain the required artistic effect. In the Basle Museum are two small oil-paintings in shades of brown, which are connected as a diptych that can be shut together and form a single whole. Such diptychs served for exhibition in domestic worship. Here Christ as Man of Sorrows and the Virgin as Mater Dolorosa are represented with deep feeling and with the most delicate execution. The two figures are placed in a rich and fantastic Renaissance portico; the sky which appears between the columns of the architecture has been painted blue, and with these blue patches distributed with fine artistic taste about the picture, otherwise of one colour, Holbein has enlivened it in a charming and picturesque way. The naked body of Christ is carried out with diligent accuracy. The Virgin, who looks round with hands upraised toward her suffering son, is extraordinarily good, as regards head, hands and drapery (Fig. 60 and 61). It is a peculiar circumstance that in this double picture, which is so small that it can never have been placed at a great height, the horizon is supposed to be below the level of the picture. Perhaps it should, on this ground, be regarded as a sketch or a repetition of a picture carried out on a large scale and intended for a high elevation.

In shades of brown without any additional colour are two large pictures, painted on canvas, which covered the inner sides of the doors by which the organ-case in the Minster at Basle was closed. Holbein has very ingeniously filled the peculiar shape of these doors; by his distribution of large, flowing ornaments over the irregular surface of each door he has produced an approximately symmetrical space for a picture, in which he has placed

Fig. 87. Jakob Meyer's wife Dorothea Kannegiesser. Drawing in black and coloured chalk,
study for the picture of the Madonna at Darmstadt. In the Basle Museum.
(After an original photograph by Braun, Clément & Co., Dornach (Alsace) and Paris.)

a figure of a Saint of more than the size of life on either side, while he
has filled the low space which remained between them with subjects which
had reference to the place. On the left wing stand the Emperor Henry II.,
founder of the Minster at Basle, and his wife, Cunigunde; between them is
seen the Minster itself. On the right wing stand, on one side, the Virgin
Mary, with the heavenly crown on her head and with the child Jesus,
nestling against her, in her arms; on the other side the Bishop Pantalus:
in the middle is a concert of delightful child-angels, who accompany as it
were, the strains of the Minster-organ with heavenly music. In these

Fig. 88. ANNA MEYER. Drawing in black and coloured chalk, study for the picture of the Madonna at Darmstadt. In the Basle Museum.

pictures, too, the horizon lies below the level of the ground, as must always be the case, strictly speaking, with pictures so hung that their ground-level is raised above the heads of the spectators; perhaps Holbein had learnt his observance of the laws of vision (to which little attention is paid as a rule) from the works of Mantegna, which are very conscientious in this respect. The organ-doors survived the iconoclastic outbreak — perhaps because the destroyers saw in them merely decorative works and not religious pictures.

It was not till the present century, when the old organ was replaced by a new one, that they were removed from their place and taken to the Museum. But they have been disfigured by a re-painting which took place in the 17th century, and are also damaged by wear and tear. Yet a good idea of their merits can still be obtained by studying the designs for them, which are among the drawings in the Museum; these are washed with brown water-colour, so that they suggest the colour of the large work, as well as the design (Fig. 62 and 63).

In the case of several other compositions which are carried out with great care, among Holbein's drawings in the Basle Museum, it may be, perhaps, supposed that they preserve designs for pictures which were destroyed during the outbreak of iconoclasm.

There is a little picture of the Virgin Mary, giving the breast to the infant Jesus, carried out in black-and-white water-colour on paper with a grey ground, in a setting of architecture suggested only by the outlines of two columns (Fig. 64). Then there is on the other hand, a drawing remarkable for the splendid elaboration of the architecture, in which a

Holy Family is the subject. The child Christ is making his first attempts at walking, between his mother Mary and his grandmother Anne, while in addition to the two women, the aged Joachim is looking on at the Scene. The light, is supposed to fall obliquely from the back, and the play of the numerous sharp points of light, which are vigorously put in with white pigment over the washed drawing on a red ground, gives a peculiar charm to the drawing (Fig. 65). In both these designs the horizon again lies below the level of the ground. Perhaps they are designs for wall-paintings to be placed high; that hypothesis agrees with the decorative character of the subjects and also with the slanting perspective, which, in both cases, suggests that there was a principal subject belonging to each picture, placed to the right and forming the middle part of a larger whole. Then there is another subject from the Passion of Our Lord, carried out in black-and-white on a grey ground: Christ bearing the Cross. Christ has fallen to the ground under the burden; he holds himself up with a painful effort on his hands, and looks up groaning, seeking in vain for compassion among the troop of unfeeling ruffians and indifferent spectators who form his escort (Fig. 66). We way compare with this drawing the strikingly beautiful woodcut, of which only a single impression (in the Basle Museum) is preserved and in which Christ, fallen down beneath the Cross, is represented alone, not as a character in a historical scene, but as a warning figure, whose bitter complaint, uttered by his eyes, appeals to the beholder (Fig. 67).

Nobody understands what is meant by a certain washed drawing, carefully carried out on reddish paper, which represents a nude woman, who steps forward in quick motion beside a column, holding in each hand a stone as if about to throw. In spite of the careful finish of the details, it is not a mere study from nature made for the sake of instruction; Holbein would have drawn such a study with a sharper precision. It must be another preliminary study for some painting, in which the figure perhaps formed only part of a larger composition. In any case there is an artistic interest merely in seeing a nude figure designed by Holbein (Fig. 68).

There are a number of subjects in various collections from the life of the Swiss landsknechts, thrown off with the greatest vivacity and only slightly finished, which were, perhaps, not conceived for any definite purpose but merely sketched from pleasure in the subjects. The Basle Museum possesses a really wonderful representation of a conflict between two bodies of lands-knechts; on one side the men with the long spears are striving to maintain an attitude of defence in serried ranks, from the other side they press on in a heavy mass, and in the middle there is a scuffle of the brawlers, who have broken from their ranks. This is depicted as forcibly and vividly as if the draughtsman were relating an event of his own life. The style of the execution also contributes to the force of the impression; the artist, wielding his brush rapidly and with instant precision, has kept the figures in the foreground clearly distinguishable in all the din and turmoil and has merely indicated by slight and wavering outlines those which stand further

Fig. 89. "MADONNA OF THE BURGOMASTER MEYER". In the Grand-Ducal Palace, Darmstadt.

Fig. 90. OLD COPY OF HOLBEIN'S "MADONNA OF THE BURGOMASTER MEYER".
In the Royal Picture-Gallery, Dresden.
(After a photograph by Franz Hanfstängl, Munich.)

back, and which, in fact, the spectator would not be able to see clearly, owing to the cloud of dust (Fig. 69). To the pictures of the landsknechts belongs also the representation of a ship in the Städel Institute at Frankfort. The transport, evidently drawn from actual observation, is preparing to leave the harbour, to convey a troop of armed men, whose costume is that of the Swiss army, to a distant land. The principal current of Swiss emigration at that time set towards France; Holbein, if he visited his friend Amerbach at Avignon, may easily have found an opportunity in these parts of witnessing such an occurrence as he has represented here. The sails of the ship are already inflated; a boat rows hastily up for the last time to fetch back anyone whose place is not on board. The men in the ship have done the honours of their departure from land, now they have to make quick about it and be off. The performers on drum and fife play the march of the landsknechts at the stern: the standard-bearer swings the great banner by way of salute. Among the crew a parting drink is still going round in large cans, even up to the mast-head. The draughtsman may be pardoned for making the figures rather too large to be in proportion to the construction of the ship (Fig. 70).

The wealth of Holbein's gift of invention and the speed of his production were applied with the most gratifying results to drawing on the wood. Those of his works for book-illustration which have become most widely known to the public, almost all belong to the period from 1523 to the beginning of 1526. Even if most of them were not published until later years, yet the circumstance that they were cut by Lützelburger's hand proves that they were produced at that period.

The so-called "Dance of Death" alphabet is one of the earliest of the works drawn by Holbein and cut by Lützelburger. Single letters of it appeared in books printed as early as 1524. In designing letters, which were intended to adorn the text of printed books after the pattern of the painted initials in mediaeval manuscripts, Holbein always followed the same style of arrangement. He left the letter itself, to which he always gave the proper Renaissance shape, in the classical form of the old Latin writing, without ornament; he provided decoration for it by a square design with figures, which forms the background of the letter, without any other connection between the little picture and the letter than that of the artistic harmony of the lines. He was fond of drawing whole alphabets in such a manner that the twenty-four little pictures — for U and V there was only one character, as also for I and J — formed together a connected series. So, for instance, he made one alphabet with the different callings and occupations of men in the guise of children's games, another with the merry goings-on of a rustic fair. But he won the greatest applause by the alphabet in which he took the power of death over all ranks as the theme of the pictures.

This theme was very popular. The beginnings of the so-called "Dance of Death" representations can be traced back to the 14th century. They

Fig. 91. "LAIS CORINTHIACA". Oil-painting of 1526. In the Basle Museum.
(After an original photograph by Braun, Clément & Co., Dornach (Alsace) and Paris.)

were pictures which symbolized the nothingness of all earthly things by
confronting the figures of the living with the figures of the dead — which
had once been the same as they and now possessed nothing more than
the naked hideousness of corrupt or withered corpses. In the 15th century
the Dominicans, especially, were fond of having whole series of such couples

painted on the walls in suitable places, in the portico of the church, in the cloister, or wherever else a number of people could see them; explanatory verses in popular language were written for them. In the verses the dead

Fig. 92. THE GODDESS OF LOVE. Oil-painting in the Basle Museum.
(After an original photograph by Braun, Clément & Co., Dornach (Alsace) and Paris.)

spoke to the living; in the pictures they offered them their hands. These were sermons in painting, which were to urge the spectator to ponder on his end and to point out the equality in death of all, by characterising among the persons represented all ranks, ecclesiastical and civil, from the

Elizabeth Dancy,   Margaret Giggs,   Sir John More, father   Sir Thomas More.   John More,   Henry Patteson,   Alice, second wife of
second daughter.   a relative brought   of Sir Thomas.   the son,   the jester,   Sir Thomas More.
                      up with the   Anne Cresacre, betrothed   Cecilia Heron, youngest   Margaret Roper,
                      daughters.   to John More the son.   daughter.   eldest daughter.

Fig. 93.   Sketch for the picture of the family of Sir Thomas More. Pen-drawing in the Basle Museum.
The names written beside the persons on this drawing are in the hand of Sir Thomas More, the notes on certain alterations in the composition are
by the hand of Holbein.

Fig. 94. Sir Thomas More. Drawing in black and coloured chalk. Study for the picture of More's family.
In the library of H. M. the Queen, Windsor Castle.
(After a photograph by Franz Hanfstängl, Munich.)

highest to the lowest. The series of couples formed, as it were, a procession. From this the idea was naturally developed of conceiving the whole
subject as a procession of dancers; that age was fond of a spice of humour,
even in very serious things. At a dance the musician could not be omitted.

Iudge More Sr Tho: Mores Father.

Fig. 95. SIR JOHN MORE, FATHER OF SIR THOMAS MORE. Study for the picture of More's family, drawn in black and coloured chalk. In the library of H. M. the Queen, Windsor Castle.
(After a photograph by Franz Hanfstängl, Munich.)

But the fiddler here was Death himself, imagined to be a personal being and fashioned, like the rest, as a living corpse. A series of these pictures formed a regular "Dance of Death". Basle, too, in Holbein's time possessed a famous Dance of Death, on the wall of the cemetery of the Dominican convent, which was a free imitation of a still older work in the women's

Fig. 96. WILLIAM WARHAM, ARCHBISHOP OF CANTERBURY. Drawing in black and coloured chalk, in the library of
H. M. the Queen, Windsor Castle.
(After a photograph by Franz Hanfstängl, Munich.)

convent of Klingenthal, in the suburb of Basle, across the Rhine. The
name has remained attached to the whole cycle of these subjects, although
after the beginning of the 16th century, the manner of representation under-
went important changes. In the corresponding pictures which the artists
of this period, and Holbein among them, designed, no more dead men

Fig. 97. WILLIAM WARHAM, ARCHBISHOP OF CANTERBURY. Oil-painting in the Louvre, Paris.

appear and there is no more dancing. In place of the dead men it is
Death who is the companion of the living man in every picture.

Holbein represented Death in the latest coherent form which a dead
body can assume — that of a fleshless skeleton. Here and there others, too,
had hit upon this form; for instance, Dürer, in a magnificent drawing of
the year 1505. That was a happy stroke of the artist, for nothing could
produce a more uncanny effect than a parcel of bones without any means of
motion, which, nevertheless, moved by some inexplicable force of its own.
Holbein's anatomical knowledge was certainly small. The skeletons which

Fig. 98. JOHN FISHER, BISHOP OF ROCHESTER. Drawing in black and coloured chalk in the library of
H. M. the Queen, Windsor Castle.

(After an original photograph by Braun, Clément & Co., Dornach (Alsace) and Paris.)

he drew are full of inaccuracies. But he did not design these subjects in order to make a display of scientific knowledge. He attained his artistic purpose by his defective skeletons as completely as anybody else has ever done who has made a similar attempt. He understood in a masterly way how to give the empty framework of bones the appearance of a living creature; the deep shadows of the empty eyesockets and the fleshless jaws, which seem to grin, gave him the means of conjuring up a peculiarly drastic expression of countenance which, by its variety, replaces all play of features.

Fig. 99. JOHN STOKESLEY, BISHOP OF LONDON. In the Royal picture-gallery, Windsor Castle.
(After an original photograph by Braun, Clément & Co., Dornach (Alsace) and Paris.)

His Alphabet of the Dance of Death (Fig. 71) begins in A with a reminiscence of the actual Dance of Death pictures: Death strikes up the dance-tune; there, too, Death no longer appears as a unit, for there are several skeletons. In many of the following pictures also Death works with the aid of comrades. In delirious joy, often in cruel scorn and mockery, the bony creature falls upon his prey — men of all positions in life. He seizes the pope, the emperor, the king, the cardinal, the empress, the queen, the bishop, the prince, the knight, the lady, the scholar, the merchant, the monk, the soldier, the nun, the jester and the courtesan; he pours the last draught down the drunkard's throat, springs upon the horse, behind the traveller, leads the bedesman kindly away, joins the gamblers in company with a devil, and clutches the child out of its cradle. The Last Judgment ends the series, in the letter Z.

These diminutive pictures are really great masterpieces. What a wealth of poetical invention, what a power of characterisation, what striking vividness of portrayal there is in every one of the compositions confined within such a narrow space! One can understand that the master, who had penetrated into the subject with all an artist's pleasure, must have felt a

7*

longing to treat the same subject differently, no longer in the cramped form of letters, which, besides, could only be seen by the public scattered through books, never in the sequence which he had thought out. He designed a "Dance of Death" with the purpose of publishing it as an independent work, in drawings which, indeed, were still small, but which afforded him room enough to carry out his poetical fancies farther in pictorial form and to give them still more substance and resemblance to life by spacious surroundings or landscape backgrounds, or even, if required, by the addition of subordinate persons. The drawings were, for the most part, cut by Lützelburger in a masterly style.

This woodcut Dance of Death has done more than anything else to make Holbein's name famous. It is curious that it was not published till many years after its creation. There are only five proof-copies extant (in the Basle, Berlin and London Museums, in the Print-cabinet at Carlsruhe and in the Bibliothèque Nationale at Paris), of the first edition as it was proposed: the number of the pictures here is forty, and the text is confined to headings in the German language. Of another edition, which contains a subject wanting in the first, and is distinguished from the latter by the circumstance that the headings, in which there are slight variations in the wording, are printed in gothic (or German) characters instead of the Latin characters then usually preferred, only a single copy (in the Library at Paris) is extant. The first actual publication took place in the year 1538 at Lyons, at the press of the brothers Caspar and Melchior Trechsel. This edition contains the 41 subjects, each accompanied by a text from the Bible in Latin and by some French verses, with a preface by the French publisher, dedicated to the Abbess of the Convent of St. Pierre at Lyons.

In later editions, which appeared with the verses also translated into German, there were eight additional subjects, omitted in the first edition because Lützelburger had been carried off by death before completing them, and because — according to the words of the learned French ecclesiastic who composed the preface and in it passed over Holbein and attributed all the merit of the drawing to the wood-engraver — nobody ventured to set his hand to the unfinished subjects, any more than he would think of touching the rainbow in the sky. At length, after several years, another talent was found to do tolerable justice to the abandoned enterprise. These subjects which were subsequently cut, or left partly cut and finished at a later time, are of such a kind that they could be omitted without disturbing the sequence, for they are not arranged in the traditional order according to station in life, but contain — like the letters T to X of the alphabet of the Dance of Death — subjects of independent invention, illustrating the manners of the time (Fig. 77). As regards some pieces, which were only inserted in much later editions, long after the artist's death, it appears questionable whether their introduction into the body of the work was contemplated by Holbein himself. The three first subjects of the series contain the introduction of this poem in pictures: the creation of Eve, the Fall and the expulsion from Paradise. Then Death makes his appearance on the scene; he helps Adam in tilling the earth with an indescribable expression of savage delight. The joy of Death at

Fig. 100. SIR HENRY GUILDFORD, MASTER OF THE HORSE TO HENRY VIII. Picture of 1527 in the Royal picture-gallery, Windsor Castle.
(After an original photograph by Braun, Clément & Co., Dornach (Alsace and Paris.)

mankind falling victim to him is jubilantly proclaimed on the next page by a concert of skeletons, some of which have tricked themselves out in an absurd way, in mockery. And now Death visits all classes, beginning with

Fig. 101. PORTRAIT OF A MAN UNKNOWN. In the Prado Gallery, Madrid.
(After an original photograph by Braun, Clément & Co., Dornach (Alsace) and Paris.)

pope and emperor, down to the poorest and most lowly and to the young infant. With grim humour he mixes in the affairs of men, now secretly, now openly; unrecognised, or causing widespread terror. To the king at his banquet he offers wine as cupbearer, as a trusty knight he escorts the empress, and as a dancing fool he clutches the queen in the midst of her courtly state. He carries in mockery the mitre and crozier as he drags the abbot along; adorned with a wreath like those which the young dandies used to wear at dance and banquet, he pulls the abbess over the convent-threshold; as verger he approaches the priest in the pulpit. Dancing and crowned with a wreath, accompanied by a skeleton with merry music, he mocks at an old woman who creeps along with the aid of a staff and tells her beads. He visits the physician as the companion of a patient; with a questioning look he offers a skull to the scholar; he robs the rich man of his money. Rising from the waves, he snaps the mast of a ship on the stormy sea (Fig. 73); with breastplate and mail-coat hanging loose upon him he drives the spear through the armour and body of a knight (Fig. 74). He assists as the young countess puts on her bridal apparel and walks as a drummer in front of the lord and lady (Fig. 75). Like a highwayman he falls upon the pedlar in the public road; like an over-zealous hind he drives the team of the husbandman, who walks behind the plough in a delightfully peaceful landscape (Fig. 76). Whichever of the subjects one may choose to contemplate, every one is a creation full of

Fig. 102. Nicholas Kratzer, Astronomer Royal to King Henry viii. Oil-painting of 1528.
In the Louvre, Paris.

meaning and full of wit, over which one may ponder for a long time. As
a noticeable sign of the times one may see on many of the pages how
the humorous features are being transformed into satire. One sees, too,
a reflection of the very events of the day; for instance, in the picture of
the pope, whom death snatches away when engaged in the task which is
the supreme manifestation of his power, while a devil stands ready to receive

his soul, the allusion to Leo X (d. 1521) is sufficiently clear; the dignified old emperor, who is interrupted in the administration of justice (Fig. 72), is unmistakeably Maximilian (d. 1519), and the king bears the features of Francis I of France, although the latter was still alive; the count, whom Death approaches in the costume of a peasant to beat him down with his

Fig. 103. SIR THOMAS GODSALVE AND HIS SON JOHN. Oil-painting of 1528.
In the Royal picture-gallery, Dresden.
(After a photograph by Franz Hanfstängl, Munich.)

own scutcheon, and the councillor, whom Death calls away while he is refusing to give hearing to a man of low estate, remind us of the peasant insurrection which raged at the very door of Basle in 1525, and of the causes which led to it. The series ends with the universal Last Judgment (Fig. 78) and with a concluding page which displays the arms of Death: a death's head on a shield with rents in it, an hour-glass and two raised bony arms as crest (Fig. 79). That the Lord Death had his proper coat-of-

Fig. 104. SIR BRYAN TUKE. Oil-painting in the Royal picture-gallery, Munich.
(After a photograph by Franz Hanfstängl, Munich.)

arms, was an established notion, which had furnished Dürer, too, with a
suggestion for one of his engravings.

In the same publisher's office, and also not till the year 1538, appeared
the largest series of cuts drawn by Holbein — his illustrations to the Old

Fig. 105. PORTRAIT OF AN ENGLISH LADY. Drawing in black and coloured chalk,
in the Basle Museum.
(After an original photograph by Braun, Clément & Co., Dornach (Alsace) and Paris.)

Testament. That these cuts, too, were produced, at least for the most part, in the years 1523 to 1526, is proved by the fact, that the hand of Lützelburger can be recognised in the cutting of the majority; those which were cut by another hand occur, curiously enough, among the first.

Trechsel's publication did not present the drawings, as was probably the original intention, in the text of an edition of the Bible, but as an independent book of pictures. Every page was accompanied by a quotation of the passage of scripture to which it belonged and a short explanation in French verse. There was, also, a preface in Latin verse; in this Holbein's name was not ignored, as it had been in the publication of the Dance of Death; on the contrary, the artist, who had to put up with his name appearing for the sake of the metre in the stunted form of Holbius, was exalted above Apelles and the other famous painters of ancient Greece. The author of the preface was an acquaintance and admirer of Holbein in person. In the same year as the first issue of the picture-book, which went through repeated later editions, the drawings also appeared in a Latin edition of the Bible which was produced by another printer at Lyons, Hugo a Porta. In this rare edition a few subjects are omitted; on the other hand, there is one, the Fall, which is wanting in the first issue, and only occurs elsewhere as a proof-impression in the Museum at Basle. Holbein's cuts for the Old

Fig. 106. PORTRAIT OF A MAN UNKNOWN. Drawing in black, red and brown chalk,
in the Basle Museum.
(After an original photograph by Braun, Clément & Co., Dornach (Alsace) and Paris.)

Testament are, in general, much less known than his Dance of Death.   But
these 91 little pictures — the form here, too, is quite small — deserve the
greatest attention.   While the artist in his other work surprises and enthrals
the attention by his witty ideas, here he keeps simply and faithfully to
the words of the text which he has to illustrate.   He reveals himself as a
narrator of the first order, who can tell everything of importance in each
subject with the most charming simplicity and naturalness, and within the
briefest limits, while he forgets nothing which belongs essentially to the story,
and avoids every superfluity (Fig. 80—85).

Among the cuts by Lützelburger is one of which very few impressions
have been preserved, which has evidently served as a head-piece to adorn
a broadside, a satirical publication on the side of the Reformers, which may
have been suppressed by the magistracy of Basle on account of its bitterness.
It represents, in the right half of the composition, a decorated hall in
which the people throng to buy the indulgences issued by the pope on his
throne, whose personality is identified by the arms of the Medici, which
are introduced everywhere; but, to the left, we see out in the open air David,
Manasseh and the poor publican as representatives of true penitents, and
God the Father stretching out his arms from Heaven down towards them.

A design of a similar kind, which also betrays Lützelburger's hand in the fine execution of the cutting, appeared as the head-piece of the Evangelical Calendar of Dr. Johannes Copp, which was printed in 1527. The design shows Christ as the true light which irradiates the world and draws the faithful to it, while the pope and his clergy turn their backs on it — to follow the guidance of the pagan philosophers, Plato and Aristotle, and fall into the pit.

The ecclesiastical contest in which the artist engaged by publishing these woodcuts, assumed an acute form in Basle. Everyone was fired with religious party-zeal. The arts, consequently, grew cold, as Erasmus puts it in one of his letters. A party established itself which was decidedly hostile to pictures. In January 1526 the guild of painters presented a petition to the council that it would graciously enable them, who had their wives and children to support as well as others, to remain at Basle. Holbein's earnings, too, had fallen off. How little use the government of Basle had for his art may be seen from the accounts of the Council, in which the only mention of a payment to Holbein during these years is of a paltry sum which he received in March 1526 for painting "certain shields in the borough of Waldenburg", perhaps the arms of the magistracy on public buildings in this town, which belonged to the district of Basle.

Yet it was probably in this very year that Holbein obtained a commission from his old patron, Jakob Meyer, in the carrying out of which he produced a work which is, without doubt, the most beautiful of all his extant religious pictures.

Jakob Meyer, "of the Hare", who had held the office of Burgomaster for the last time in the year 1521, was a firm adherent of the old church, while the Reformation was steadily gaining the upper hand at Basle. So, precisely at the time when the Catholic party was hardly able to hold its ground any longer in the Council, he had a picture painted which was obviously intended to be set up over the altar of a chapel, and in so doing made, as it were, a public profession of faith. He had himself portrayed with his whole family, placed under the patronage and protection of the Virgin Mary. In carrying out this commission Holbein produced the splendid picture of the Virgin which is now in the possession of the Grand Duke of Hesse, and is kept in the Grand-ducal palace at Darmstadt.

Of Holbein's preliminary studies for this painting, the portrait-sketches of Jakob Meyer, his wife Dorothea and their daughter Anna are preserved. These three drawings, carried out in the well-known manner of the artist in black chalk with the assistance of a few coloured crayons, are in the Basle Museum. The head of the husband (Fig. 86), in black and red on a background of yellowish tone, is quite slightly treated but most telling and effective; the expression, even, which he was to have in the painting, is already indicated. The head of the wife (Fig. 87) is more closely veiled by the face-band than the painter subsequently chose to make it in carrying out the picture; the suggestions of colour are confined to the red in the face and a little brown to indicate the hair, which shows through the cap, and the fur-lining to the collar of the mantle. Anna Meyer (Fig. 88), whose age, about thirteen years, is one of the points which help to decide the

Fig. 107. HOLBEIN'S WIFE AND CHILDREN. Oil-painting on paper. In the Basle Museum.
(After an original photograph by Braun, Clément & Co., Dornach (Alsace) and Paris.)

date of the picture, is drawn at once as a half-length, with her arms approximately in the position which they were to have in the picture; the face with its delicate flesh-tint, the golden-brown hair, the colour of which was produced by drawing yellow and brown one over the other, and the

Fig. 108. Designs for metal dagger-sheahs.
Pen-drawings in the Basle Museum.

white costume, enlivened by a red girdle and by ornaments on the collar touched-in with yellow, stand out with almost the effect of a finished picture from a background slightly washed with green. The young girl appears decidedly to more advantage in the drawing than in the picture; that is principally because her uncovered hair is much more becoming to her than the gala head-dress, used perhaps on some special occasion, such as the first communion, which conceals the greater part of the head, on which the hair was piled up in curls.

The painting itself (Fig. 89), of three quarters the size of life, is one of the rare works of art which dominate the beholder at first sight with the full power of a perfect art and which, once seen, are never forgotten.

The Queen of Heaven does not here appear on her throne, but stands erect in the midst of the donor's family, over whom her mantle is spread out; the Divine Child lays his head close against his mother's breast and stretches out his little hand over the suppliants in benediction. On one side kneels Jakob Meyer in fervent prayer, next to him his son aged about twelve, whose devotions are somewhat disturbed by the youngest member of the family, a delightful little naked child who does not trouble himself at all at present about heavenly things, and has to be kept steady with both hands by his brother. On the opposite side kneel the first and the second wife of the Burgomaster as well as the only daughter, in quiet and earnest devotion; the latter's attention appears to be divided between the rosary in her hands and her dear little brother. Meyer's head is a marvel of expression: the deep and genuine piety of a man who seeks in trustful prayer for calm in encountering the bitterness which the outer world and his own unruly spirit have in store for him; and how well the fingers,

Fig. 109. Dagger-sheath with the Dance of Death.
Design for silversmith's work. Washed drawing in the Basle Museum.

Fig. 110. ORNAMENTAL FRIEZE. Washed drawing in the Basle Museum.

closely pressed together, correspond with the tension of the muscles of the
face! And then how this expression is emphasised by the contrast of the
innocent faces of the boys! The effect of the two women side by side is
very curious: one who is still quite in the midst of life, in whose healthy,
mobile face one can trace the indefatigable energy of the active housewife,
and one long since dead, who belongs no more to this world, who gives
one the impression of being stiff and immoveable from the straight profile
in which her head and figure appear, and of whose face (which Holbein
had never seen) only a small piece peers out from the band which veils it,
as if from grave-clothes. It produces a curious effect, too, to see only the
tips of the fingers of the folded hands of the women, including the daughter.
Over the faces of these people with their various emotions is the countenance of the Mother of Grace with its heavenly tranquillity, a countenance
which, in its simplicity of form and expression, is the offspring of such
seriousness and depth of feeling in the artist that it will bear comparison
even with the master-pieces of the pious fifteenth century painters. The infant
Jesus looks at the spectator with his face only half turned towards him
and a pained expression, as if he had just been crying. That is surely not
the painter's idea, but the donor's — to make the Redeemer give expression
in this way to his sorrow at the condition of the church at Basle. The
artist must be credited with the idea of making the child give the blessing
with the left hand; if the painter had made the child raise his right hand
he would have had to relinquish a motive, which does much to heighten
the impression which the patron wished him to suggest—the motive of the
child leaning back, as if weary.

In 1887 the picture, which had been retouched in many places in an
arbitrary manner, was cleaned by a skilful hand, and it has reappeared from
beneath the spurious layer of paint in a surprisingly perfect state of preservation, so that in this masterpiece of Holbein we can give our full
admiration to the splendour of his colouring, which is here as fresh as if
the picture had just left the easel. The bright point which forms the
nucleus of the enchanting scheme of colour is the face of Mary, quite
light in tone, with rosy cheeks. The fair hair, which encloses this face
under the golden crown set with pearls and a gem of reddish-violet colour,
is soft and marvellously fine; the glistening curls and the scattered hairs
which cling to the mantle are rendered with unique skill; it is all painted
with the utmost delight an artist can feel; Dürer never drew the single
hairs with greater delicacy, but here the hair, as a whole, is also rendered
with picturesque effect. The head of the Virgin with its golden setting
and with the fair, curly head of the infant Jesus, whose body carries on

the light tint of the face to the Virgin's hands, so that all these delicate flesh-tints form a single unit of light, has for background the shiny tone of the shell-shaped canopy of a niche, made of highly-polished reddish-brown marble. The other part of the niche consists of a grey stone, the colour of which forms a transition in quiet tones to the blue of the sky, which appears at the side, intersected by the green boughs of a fig-tree. The Virgin's dress is dark, greenish-blue, with the lower part of the sleeves of the colour of gold, in which, as in all the ornamental parts, actual gold is employed in the painting; the large, dark mass of the robe, the shadows of which run into the unlighted inner side of the greenish-grey mantle, is interrupted by a bright red girdle; at the wrists a narrow strip of white material appears, and along the hem of the bodice a thin, veil-like stuff lies between dress and neck. The group to the right of the Virgin passes from deep black (which is the colour of Meyer's hair and of his overcoat, made of material of a *moiré* pattern and lined with light brown fur) through intermediate tones of colour in the costume of the elder boy, to the light tint of the baby's flesh, which is as high in tone as the body of Christ; the elder boy, with brown curls, wears a light-brown coat trimmed with reddish-brown velvet, with golden clasps and tags on thin, blue strings, and hose of cinnabar-red; on his girdle hangs a yellowish-green purse with dull-blue silk tassels. There is a corresponding gradation in the three faces: the high colour of Meyer's complexion, with traces of blue on the shaven chin, the fresh

Fig. 111. PANEL complexion of the boy and the delicate face of the child. In
OF ORNAMENT.
Washed drawing the group of women there are only a few spots of colour between
in the Basle
Museum. black and white, besides the face of the living wife, which
gives twice the effect of colour, surrounded as it is by nothing but white; the head-band of Anna Meyer consists of gold material richly embroidered with pearls, crimson silk tassels hang over the brown braids of hair; on the top of the band lies a little wreath of white and red flowers with a few green leaves; the rosary in Anna's hands is red. The carpet, which falls in front over a low step, has a pattern of red and green with some black and white on a deep-yellow ground; its general tone is very warm. The description of the colours of a picture can really give no notion of the impression which they produce. The impression which the colours of the Darmstadt picture make on one's mind is like that of listening to a peal of church bells.

It is in the colour and the effect which it has on the temperament of the beholder that the greatest difference lies between the original painting of the Madonna of the Burgomaster Meyer and the copy of it which is in the Dresden Gallery — a copy painted at a date not known, but so cleverly

Fig. 112. ERASMUS OF ROTTERDAM.
Woodcut frontispiece to the works of Erasmus.

From the rare first issne with the inscription below:

If anyone has not seen Erasmus in his bodily shape,
This plate, drawn skilfully from life presents his counterfeit.

that it passed for more than a century as the original. But the difference
is not in the colour only. Even the photographic reproduction shows how
much the composition has lost in sincerity by the copyist thinking it
necessary to alter the thickset figure of the Virgin as Holbein painted it to
slimmer proportions, and by making the niche higher, from a similar mistaken
idea of beauty; it shows, too, how the heads have lost their force of
character at the hand of the copyist (Fig. 90).

Two idealized portraits of a young lady, in the Basle Museum, one of
which bears the date 1526, were, perhaps, not painted to order, but rather
for the artist's own amusement in the spare time which was left to him in

Fig. 113. PHILIP MELANCHTHON. Miniature-painting in oils.
In the Royal picture-gallery, Hanover.

consequence of the hostility to pictures which prevailed at that date. The
paintings, carried out with exquisite delicacy on a small scale — about one-
third of the size of life — represent with an almost identical effect of
colouring the young blonde, whose fair complexion has a somewhat dull
tone, at half-length, in a dress of dark-red velvet slashed and tied with
gold laces, showing white puffs and wide upper sleeves of dark-golden silk;
she sits behind a parapet of grey stone, and at her back a dark green
curtain hangs down in broad folds. In one picture we see a little heap of
gold pieces lying on the ledge of the parapet; the lady holds out her right
hand open towards the spectator, as if to receive more, while her left hand
rests in the folds of a blue mantle, which lies across her lap; she looks
before her with downcast eyes, and a deep and quiet sorrow lies in the

expression of the refined face. On the front of the ledge are the words
"Lais Corinthiaca. 1526", as if chiselled in the stone (Fig. 91). The other
picture is distinguished from the first, as regards the costume, by having a
black cap ornamented with a little gold on the hair instead of the gold
cap in the first portrait, and by letting the fore-arms appear uncovered
from the upper sleeves of yellow silk. In this the beauty looks at the
spectator with a smile, whilst her hand moves to greet and welcome him;
a cupid, resting on her knee, leans over the stone parapet — a dear little
red-haired rogue, who holds an arrow in his tiny hand (Fig. 92). The sense
of the two paintings is explained by their juxtaposition: the gold which

Fig. 114. ERASMUS OF ROTTERDAM. Miniature-painting in oils. In the Basle Museum.
(After an original photograph by Braun, Clément & Co., Dornach (Alsace) and Paris.

she desired cannot make the young woman happy; love alone can do so.
As to the relations of Holbein with the person whom he portrayed in this
way, the inscription "Lais Corinthiaca" hardly leaves a doubt. The courtesan,
Lais of Corinth, famous for her seductive beauty, was the mistress of Apelles;
and to be called Apelles was just as usual for Holbein as for other painters
of that period who were surrounded by learned admirers. The name of the
lady is betrayed by the old catalogue of the Amerbach collection; she was
a daughter of the noble family of Offenburg.

As early as the year 1524 Erasmus of Rotterdam had thought of pro-
curing for his young friend, whose earnings at Basle were in no way
proportionate to his eminent gifts, a more profitable field of industry, by

8*

recommending him to his friends in England. And Thomas More, the
great statesman and scholar who, a few years later, became Lord Chancellor
of England, promised in his reply to Erasmus that he would do all in his
power for the painter, in whom he had recognised "a marvellous artist"
by the specimens of his work which had come from abroad. Since the
condition of affairs at Basle made the outlook for art more and more gloomy,
Holbein resolved to follow his patron's advice, and left Basle towards the
autumn of 1526, in order to travel to England by way of Antwerp.

As a friend of Erasmus, Holbein was received as a cherished guest in
Sir Thomas More's house at Chelsea. As an artist he was not wholly
unknown here, even before Erasmus sent More his own portrait painted by
him; for in the edition of More's book, "Utopia", of world-wide circulation,

Fig. 115. KING REHOBOAM AND THE DEPUTIES OF THE PEOPLE. Washed drawing, partly tinted design for
a wall-painting in the Basle Town-hall. In the Basle Museum.
(After an original photograph by Braun, Clément & Co., Dornach (Alsace) and Paris.)

which Froben got up in 1518, the dedication-page was adorned by the
border which Holbein designed in 1515 and signed with his name.

Through the recommendation of his distinguished host, Holbein found
ample occupation as a portrait-painter. First, of course, he painted Sir
Thomas More himself. Out of many portraits called by this name and
attributed to Holbein, a half-length figure in a private collection in London,
with the date 1527, passes as the only one which is authentic. He painted
More's whole family, the size of life, in a large picture, in tempera, on canvas.
This much-admired picture has disappeared and left no trace behind it.
But the Basle Museum possesses a sketch for it, a clever pen-drawing in
outline (Fig. 93). Sir Thomas More sent this drawing, on which he wrote
the name of each person by the side of the likeness so ably suggested in
a few strokes, by the hand of the artist himself, when he returned, as a
present to Erasmus. Of the drawings carried out on the scale of the

finished picture, in which Holbein took the likenesses of the several heads
for the family group, most are, fortunately, preserved; they are in the
Royal library at Windsor Castle (Fig. 94, the head of Sir Thomas More,
and Fig. 95, that of his father).

Among the first persons, probably, whose portraits Holbein painted in
England, were the eminent ecclesiastical friends and patrons of Erasmus;
Warham, Archbishop of Canterbury, and Fisher, Bishop of Rochester. The
drawings for these two portraits are also at Windsor Castle (Fig. 96 and 98).
Of the portrait of Warham, two versions, both original, are extant, one of
which is still in the archiepiscopal palace at Lambeth, the other in the
Louvre (Fig. 97). Next to the portraits of the two aged churchmen comes
that of a younger man, Stokesley, Bishop of London, in the picture-gallery
of Windsor Castle (Fig. 99). The same collection is adorned by a master-
piece of the year 1527, the portrait of Sir Henry Guildford, Master of the

Fig. 116. SAMUEL ANNOUNCING TO SAUL THE WRATH OF GOD. Washed drawing, partly coloured
design for a wall-painting in the Basle Town-hall. In the Basle Museum.

Horse to King Henry VIII. This chivalrous gentleman, a friend of More's
and also acquainted with Erasmus, who had borne the banner of his sovereign
in battle in the campaign against France, stands in rich ceremonial costume,
with an inner garment of gold brocade under the black surcoat trimmed
with fur, decorated with the collar of the order of the Garter and holding
the chamberlain's wand in his hand (Fig. 100). A splendid piece of painting,
which, it may be inferred from the costume, was produced during Holbein's
first visit to England, is the portrait in the Prado Gallery at Madrid of an
old gentleman dressed in black with a very red complexion and an unusually
large nose (Fig. 101). The date 1528 is on the excellent portrait, in the
Louvre, of the Astronomer Royal, Nicholas Kratzer of Munich, a half-length
of the size of life, surrounded by scientific instruments, which are painted
with extreme accuracy (Fig. 102). Germany possesses a work of 1528,
the small double portrait of Thomas Godsalve and his son John, in the
Dresden Gallery (Fig. 103). The badly preserved portrait of Sir Bryan Tuke
in the Munich Gallery also probably belongs to this period — a portrait in

which the person, taking the idea perhaps from Holbein's designs of the
Dance of Death, had Death represented by his side, approaching from the
back as a skeleton with a scythe in his hand, and pointing to the hour-glass,
nearly spent, upon the table (Fig. 104).

In portrait-painting Holbein still kept up, both now and later, the practice
which he had adopted from the beginning. He based the picture on a
drawing carried out on paper, in which he made a few notes of colour
with coloured chalks, sufficient for him to carry on the picture so far that
the model only had to sit again for the last finish. Among the drawings in
the Basle Museum which are derived from Amerbach's collection are some
portrait-drawings from England, which the painter brought back home with
him, either after his first sojourn in England or on his second return.
These are the portraits of a distinguished husband and wife sketched in
rapid outlines with light flesh-tints, a rather more finished portrait of the
royal Master of the Horse, Sir Nicholas Carew, and the particularly fine
portrait of an unknown lady in the peculiar head-dress of the English
fashion at that time (Fig. 105). Next to these portrait-drawings may
be mentioned that of a young man unknown, who, to judge by the type
of his face, is not an Englishman but a German — the finest of all Holbein's
portrait-drawings at Basle. In this grand specimen of masterly drawing the
face under the wide-brimmed hat, which is shaded with black laid on in strokes
and rubbed in, is carried out so as to give the complete effect of painted
flesh-tints, and this merely with red and black in the simplest way imaginable;
the hair is drawn in a strong, brown tone, which suggests even the modelling of the wavy hair, and the fur-trimming of the coat-collar is slightly,
but sufficiently, indicated with the same brown pencil (Fig. 106). Another
likeness carried out by a different kind of process, painting in body-colour,
also a masterpiece of the first order, belongs to a German collection; this
is the head of an unknown man with a beard, in the Berlin Print-Cabinet
(Frontispiece).

In the summer of 1528 Holbein was once more at Basle. The success
which had followed his journey to England is proved by the fact that
immediately after his return he bought a house; at a later date he also
bought a smaller house adjoining it.

One of his first tasks after his return home may have been the picture
of his own family, which is one of the most fascinating objects in the Basle
Museum to the modern visitor. We see Dame Elsbeth with two children,
a fair-haired boy and a little girl with red hair (Fig. 107). The children
are, doubtless, the two eldest, Philip and Catherine. Of Philip we learn
that he was "a good, well-behaved lad"; he became a goldsmith, travelled
much after his apprenticeship at Paris and finally settled at Augsburg,
where he founded the branch of the family on which the Emperor Matthias
conferred a patent of nobility as the Holbeins of Holbeinsberg. After
Philip and Catherine came two other children: James, who died as a goldsmith at London, and Küngolt, who married at Basle, like her elder sister.

The picture, painted the size of life in oils on paper, which was subsequently cut out along the outlines and mounted on a panel, is a masterpiece of exquisite painting and a wonderful piece of artistic copying from nature.

Fig. 117. GEORGE GISSE, MERCHANT OF THE STEELYARD, LONDON. Oil-painting of 1532. In the Royal Museum, Berlin.
(After a photograph by Franz Hanfstängl, Munich.)

This realism attains to the simplicity of nature herself. It looks as if the painter had taken the three figures just as chance put them before him, and yet how well-balanced and proportioned is the work of art! A woman past the prime of life with a sad expression, two nice-looking, healthy, children with nothing particularly attractive about them, all these in extremely plain dress — the woman's dress, cut low according to the fashion of the

time at Basle and without ornament, is dark-green; a strip of thin, brown
fur along an outer garment of the same colour as the dress and a very
thin veil over the light-brown hair, covered at the back of the head by a
reddish-brown cap, are the only pieces of ornament; the boy has a very
dark greenish-blue jacket and the girl a frock of light undyed wool — that
is what Holbein has made into a picture perfectly beautiful in the proportions of light and shade, in the flow of the lines and in the harmony of
the colours.

One would think that the painter who could show such a likeness to
his fellow-citizens must have been overwhelmed with orders for portraits.
But the people of Basle were entirely occupied with the religious conflict,
and the blind zeal of parties drowned the voice of the council, which recommended that "no man should call another papist or lutheran, heretic,
adherent of the new faith or of the old, but each should be left unharassed
and unscorned in his own belief". How could a citizen at such a time
give his attention to the arts of peace and beauty?

The date 1529 on a drawing in the Basle Museum brings us to a
subordinate but extremely meritorious branch of Holbein's work, his practice
as an inventor of patterns for art-handicraft. Whereas in his early youth
it was principally the glasier's craft that he furnished with patterns, at a
later period he preferred to make designs for goldsmith's work. The
aforesaid date is on a design, drawn with the pen and washed, for a dagger-
sheath covered with splendid Renaissance ornament (Fig. 108). The Basle
Museum possesses, besides this, four other preliminary drawings by Holbein,
each more beautiful than the last, for ornate dagger-sheaths, as worn by
dandies and men of high rank. One, very rich and in exquisite taste,
contains, merely sketched in outline with the pen, three mythological subjects, in compartments one above the other, the judgment of Paris, Pyramus
and Thisbe and Venus and Cupid and, below these, a head between ornaments
(Fig. 108). The three others are also decorated with figure-subjects, so
arranged, according to the favourite mode of carrying the dagger suspended
horizontally from the girdle, that the compositions run along the surface
lengthways, from the tip of the sheath to the hilt of the dagger. In one
of the drawings, in which the mere outline is sketched, there is a Roman
triumphal procession; in the second, carried out in wash with the most
delicate and subtle modelling, the subject is the crossing of the Jordan by
the Israelites; the third contains a Dance of Death: king and queen, warrior
and monk, wife and child are compelled to follow the skeletons, who skip
along in mocking glee (Fig. 109). Next to the dagger-sheaths we may
mention the strips of ornament, now upright, now horizontal, which could
be applied in several branches of art-handicraft, but were calculated principally for execution in goldsmith's work. Of these the Basle Museum
contains a humorous frieze with nude children, another, more highly finished,
with children hunting and playing between the grand curves of the ornament (Fig. 110), and an upright panel in which there is an amusing series

Fig. 118. Portrait of a German Merchant in London, 1532. In the Schönborn Gallery, Vienna.

of bears climbing up the branches of a vine, accompanied by a man per-
forming on drum and fife (Fig. 111).

Holbein's taste in designing ornamental motives, which had shown itself
so rich and fertile at an early date, was not arrested in its development.
The best example of the gradual refinement of his taste, and, at the same
time, a proof that he kept pace with the Renaissance style in its advance

Fig. 119. A MERCHANT OF THE STEELYARD, LONDON. Oil-painting of 1532,
in the collection at Windsor Castle.
(After an original photograph by Braun, Clément & Co., Dornach
(Alsace) and Paris.)

and modification, is a splendid woodcut, which must have been produced at this time (Fig. 112); "Erasmus of Rotterdam in a frame-work" (Gehäus) is the name of the piece in Amerbach's catalogue, which includes woodcuts. This frame, decorative and rich and yet pure and distinguished in its forms, is, perhaps, the most beautiful thing that was produced in that period at all in the way of decoration for books. But the portrait of Erasmus which it encloses is just as great a masterpiece as the frame itself. Here we see the wit and scholar at whole length: a weakly figure clad in a long robe or gown lined with fur, and yet with a grandeur and significance, not only in the head, which looks towards the spectator, but also in the whole attitude. He rests his right hand on the head of a truncated statue of Terminus, supposed to be alive, and points to this figure with a gesture of his left hand. Terminus, the deity who protected established ways and boundaries, had been chosen by Erasmus as a symbol of his efforts as a writer. The full significance of this symbol is communicated to us by a washed drawing in the Basle Museum, which Holbein had made at some time for Erasmus — apparently for the purpose of being carried out in painted glass. Terminus, framed in an arch supported by columns, stands in a wide landscape, to which a few spots of green colouring give a lively and effective appearance; the head of the statue, surrounded by a halo of rays, turns slightly aside and utters, casually as it may seem, and yet with incontrovertible decision, the words written at the side: "Concedo nulli" (I yield to no man). Holbein understood his learned friend. The whole composition has a remarkably grand effect, and the speaking expression of the face of the god Terminus is a masterpiece of the highest order. The woodcut of Erasmus in the frame, was designed as frontispiece to the works of Erasmus. The

Fig. 120.   DERICH TYBIS OF DUISBURG, MERCHANT IN LONDON.   Oil-painting in the Imperial Gallery, Vienna.
(After a photograph by J. Löwy, Vienna.)

rare first impressions have a Latin inscription in two lines at the foot,
praising the excellence of the likeness. In the later edition, which appeared
in 1540, as title-page to the collected edition of the writings of Erasmus

which was got up by Hieronymus, the son of Johannes Froben, there are
two distichs instead of one only, in which the draughtsman is named in
terms as complimentary as the author, who had died four years before this
edition of his collected works was published.

This design was one of the last which Holbein did for the Basle printers.
In the years which preceded his journey to England he had designed a
few more allegorical title-pages for theological writings. Now, it appears,
the opposition to pictures went so far that even an ornament of this kind
in a religious book was thought questionable. Only one further cut belongs
to this later period, a representation of St. Paul in an architectural frame
of similar style to that of the portraits of Erasmus.

It goes without saying that at this time there was no longer any
opportunity at Basle of painting pictures for churches. As early as Easter
1528 all the pictures had been removed from several churches; in the
following year there was a furious outbreak of iconoclasm. The Council
was incapable of withstanding the fanatics. A decree was passed against
setting up religious pictures in churches.

Such rude proceedings were an abomination to the fine feelings of
Erasmus, who has left vivid narratives of the occurrences of that time.
He resolved, heavy at heart, to quit the town which had endeared itself
to him as "the peaceful abode of the Muses", and in which he had resided
permanently since 1521. Accompanied by Bonifacius Amerbach, he retired
to Freiburg. His friend, the artist, must have visited him there, for a small
portrait of Erasmus painted by Holbein — the head in three-quarter face,
the hands resting on a book which lies open on the table — is dated 1530.
The original portrait is in the picture-gallery at Parma; there are copies
of it in various collections. There is the same view of the head in a
precious little round picture, only four inches in diameter, in the Basle
Museum, a bust in black clothes with brown fur on a greenish-blue background (Fig. 114).

A pendant, apparently, to the miniature-portrait of Erasmus is a likeness of Melanchthon (Fig. 113) carried out with equal delicacy, which
belongs to the Royal picture-gallery at Hanover, and is still in the original
case, with decorative paintings in grisaille upon it.

In the summer of 1530 it at last occurred to the Council of Basle
that they still had at their disposal an opportunity of finding work for a
painter of the importance and wide-spread fame of Holbein. They gave
him a commission to paint that wall of the Council-chamber in the town-
hall which had been left without decoration eight years before. This time the
subjects were chosen, according to the change in the spirit of the age,
not from classical, but from biblical history. One of the two large paintings
with which Holbein covered the wall in question represented king Rehoboam
spurning with a harsh answer the deputies of the people who prayed that
their yoke might be made lighter. The other represents king Saul, as he
returns from the campaign against the Amalekites and hears from Samuel

Fig. 121. PORTRAIT OF A GERMAN RESIDENT IN LONDON, 1533. In the Royal Museum, Berlin.
(After a photograph by Franz Hanfstängl, Munich.)

that he has been rejected for his disobedience to God's command. Though the wall-paintings themselves perished from damp before the 16th century had expired, we can recognise in the extant designs for both pictures (in the Basle Museum) how magnificently Holbein performed his task; they show that he must also be reckoned among the greatest masters as a painter on a monumental scale.

Rehoboam is represented on the throne, in a rich portico; behind him sit his councillors on both sides, the old, whose advice he has neglected, and the young, whom he follows — to the hurt of his kingdom. Before him stand the dignified and aged deputies, confounded by the king's words and, in part, already turning to leave his presence, for he has just declared to them in great wrath: "My little finger shall be thicker than my father's loins; my father chastised you with whips, but I will chastise you with scorpions". By a very simply conceived, but highly expressive, play of gesture the artist has given a symbolical rendering of these words of the king: Rehoboam stretches out the little finger of the clenched fist which he shakes menacingly at the envoys, and with the other hand he points scornfully, without raising his arm from the side of the throne, at the scourge in the hand of a page who stands on the steps of the throne. Outside the portico we see in the background the sequel of the obstinate harshness of the ruler; the revolt of a portion of the people, symbolised by the coronation of the rival king, Jeroboam (Fig. 115). In transferring the design to a large scale the master deviated in essential points from this sketch, which is carried out as a washed drawing, with some indication of colour, in the distance and in the sky, as seen through the windows, in the flesh-tints and a few other places. This may be seen by the remains of the wall-painting, which have been discovered in some sort of preservation and placed in the Museum. Among these remnants are the head and the raised hand of Rehoboam with the little finger stretched out; the head, a masterpiece of strong expression, is not, as in the sketch, seen from the front, but from the side, in sharp profile. In correspondence with this attitude of the king is a very fine group of heads of anxious listeners, which has also been preserved.

There is no question that the artist found a means of making the impression more vivid by placing the speaker and the audience opposite to one another in profile; if for no other reason, because it was possible for him in this way to show the faces of those deputies also who are not yet turning away from the king. It is worth observing that the small remnants inform us that Holbein did not disdain the use of gilding, even in wall-paintings.

The extant sketch for the other wall-painting is rather more finished than that for the picture of Rehoboam, which was not strictly adhered to. The perfect balance of the composition, which could not have been improved upon by any alteration, entitles us to the supposition that it was preserved in all essentials, without change. It is a massive picture (Fig. 116). We see the victorious army, with both horse and foot in antique armour, returning with the captive king of the Amalekites. The castles and towns devastated by the war are still burning. The herds, for the sake of which the conqueror has transgressed the divine command, are being driven up from the distance. King Saul marches at the head of his warriors; he has dismounted to give a reverential greeting to the prophet Samuel. The latter, however, comes to meet him with his right arm extended in menace; it seems as if we

must hear the mighty utterance with which he dashes the pride of the
conqueror: "Hath the Lord as great delight in burnt offerings and sacrifices,
as in obeying the voice of the Lord? . . . . Because thou hast rejected the
word of the Lord, he hath also rejected thee from being king." The form
of this one man is so mighty in conception that it counterbalances the whole
army which is marching towards him. A tablet to contain the words of
Samuel, in which the subject and the significant lesson of the picture were

Fig. 122. ROBERT CHESEMAN, FALCONER TO KING HENRY VIII.
Painting of 1533, in the Royal picture-gallery at the Hague.
(After an original photograph by Braun, Clément & Co., Dornach (Alsace) and Paris.)

declared, is indicated in the sketch. We have to suppose the tablet with
the inscription to be suspended from the beam of the architecture forming
the frame, one pillar of which is included in the sketch. The presence of
this suggestion of the accessories is another argument for believing that
Holbein adhered to this design when carrying out the painting. Here, again,
we get no idea of the colouring of the picture, for the suggestions of colour
in the design are confined to blue in the sky, in the distant mountains and
in a stream of water which traverses the plain, red in the conflagration
and a brownish wash in the tract of country, which in certain places, as

Nicholas Borbonius Poeta.

Fig. 123. THE POET NICOLAS BOURBON DE VANDOEUVRE. Drawing in black and
coloured chalk. In the library of H. M. the Queen, Windsor Castle.
(After a photograph by Franz Hanfstängl, Munich.)

in the small tree in the middle-distance, combines with a blue tone to form green. These notes of colour hardly serve any purpose except to break up the background and to make the figures stand out in special prominence. The figures themselves are drawn in brown and shaded with a wash of cold, grey tone.

This one large piece of work was hardly enough to compensate the master for the absence of other commissions.

What paltry jobs the great artist had once more to put up with is proved by an entry in the accounts of the Council of fourteen florins paid to him in the autumn of 1531 for "painting both clocks on the Rhine-Gate", The sum of fourteen florins for such a small piece of painting in the open street, appears, it is true, relatively large, when we learn that he was only paid seventy-two florins for the two large paintings in the Town-hall.

The idea of again trying his luck in England must have seemed all the more attractive to Holbein, inasmuch as his patron, Sir Thomas More, had meanwhile been promoted to the highest office in the kingdom and was conducting the affairs of state as Lord Chancellor. So he turned his back once more on Basle and travelled to London. When he was gone, the Basle Council wrote him a flattering letter and offered him a fixed salary if he would come back. But this offer came too late—for Holbein immediately found ample and remunerative occupation in London. Sir Thomas More had laid down the burden of high office in May, 1532— perhaps before Holbein's arrival. The brilliant circle to which the Lord Chancellor would have introduced him did not open its doors immediately to the artist. But he found admittance to another circle, which offered him social intercourse, combined with the language and manners of his own home, and ample opportunities for exercising his abilities. This was the company of German merchants, who resided in large numbers in London and formed a close corporation among themselves. Their place of assembly was the "Steelyard", the property of the Hanseatic League, in which warehouses and dwelling-houses were grouped round the old hall of the guild, while a special wine-shop and a well-kept garden were not lacking. In the years 1532 and 1533 Holbein painted quite a number of portraits of German merchants of the Steelyard. The finest of these, a gem of painting, is in the Berlin Museum. The young, fair-haired man portrayed in it is named George Gisse or Gyze, as the picture itself informs us (Fig. 117). We see him in his workroom, wearing a silken doublet of a cool red colour and a surcoat of black cloth, which shows the delicate folds of the shirt in front of the neck above the low-cut inner garment, and with a black cloth cap on his head. He is surrounded by all the little things of daily use, arranged, as he was accustomed to have them, ready to his hand, on the table covered with a handsome cloth in front of him, and on the wooden shelves, set up against the wall of painted green wood-work. A number of letters are stuck behind rails which run along the wall, as well as writing-paper and narrow strips for tying up letters. Besides the articles which he used in his business there is a shapely vase of the most delicate Venetian glass, full of water with carnations placed in it. The carnation denotes, in the language of flowers, the season of happy love; it is the special flower of bride and bridegroom. George Gisse is just engaged in opening, in his leisurely, Low-German way, a letter from home, on which we can read the address: "For the hands of the worthy George Gisse, my brother, at London in England." On the wall is written up in chalk: "Nulla sine merore voluptas" (no pleasure without grief), signed below, G. Gyze. A sheet of paper fastened higher up against the wall contains a few verses in praise of the portrait, with a note of the sitter's age (thirty-four) and the date 1532. From the point of view of painting it is not right that we should be able to decipher such fine writing at the distance at which the wall stands behind the table, the front edge of which touches the margin of the picture. But the way in which this and all the other minute details are done is simply marvellous; no painter of still-life has ever attained to a more perfect execution. This picture was doubtless one of the first, perhaps

Fig. 124. HENRY BRANDON, SON OF THE DUKE OF SUFFOLK. Miniature-portrait of 1535.
In the library of H. M. the Queen, Windsor Castle
(After a photograph by Franz Hanfstängl, Munich.)

the very first, which he painted for a member of the Steelyard, so he wished to advertise himself by a kind of master-piece, in the old sense of the word and he crowded the picture with details in which he could make a brilliant display of his dexterity. For people of a prosaic and practical turn of mind, like this worthy merchant — we read it in his

Fig. 125. KING HENRY VIII. Chalk-drawing from life. In the Royal Print-Cabinet, Munich.

features — are more capable of admiring and prizing the dexterity of an artist, which they can estimate with the understanding, than of deriving a true enjoyment of art from the artistic feeling (wherein art really consists), which can only be communicated to natures which have in themselves a fine capacity for feeling. In view of the extreme finish with which all the objects in this picture are made to appear substantial, we can perfectly understand the eulogies of those contemporaries ot the master who admired in his

Fig. 126. KING HENRY VIII. Oil-painting in the collection at Windsor Castle, agreeing with the fresco by Holbein at Whitehall, which has perished.
(After an original photograph by Braun, Clément & Co., Dornach (Alsace) and Paris.)

works before all else the illusion of the eye which they produced. But Holbein's achievement in not allowing the main point to be obscured by all this minute finish of accessories, his being able, in spite of all the petty

9*

details, to allow his own artistic feeling, his grand scheme of colour and his acute perception of the character of the person, to appeal to us—that is the most admirable thing in this marvellous picture.

The date 1532 occurs also on the portrait of a young man, conceived in a sympathetic and simple manner, in the picture-gallery of the palace of Count Schönborn at Vienna (Fig. 118), and on that of a bearded man, busied with his papers, at Windsor Castle (Fig. 119), in which it is thought, from the not very distinct incription on a letter, that the goldsmith Hans of Antwerp can be recognised. The Netherlanders also formed part of the German colony in London.

Among the portraits of the year 1533 that of Derich Tybis of Duisburg, in the Imperial Gallery at Vienna (Fig. 120), and that of an unknown man with a fair beard, in the Royal Museum at Berlin (Fig. 121), may be specially mentioned.

A portrait of the master by himself, of this year, carried out on the scale of a miniature, is said to be in a private collection at Prague.

But it was not only portraits that Holbein painted in the Steelyard. An opportunity was also offered to him of executing a painting of monumental size. He adorned the banqueting-hall of the old house of the guild with two great allegorical pictures, which, however, he did not carry out on the wall itself, but in distemper on canvas. These represented, in processions of numerous figures in the form of a frieze, the "Triumph of Wealth" and the "Triumph of Poverty"; their didactic purport was, that riches, as well as poverty, have need of lofty virtues in order to lead to a good end. Once more there are only copies and a small sketch preserved in the Louvre at Paris, from which we can form an approximate idea of the beauty of these paintings, which were prized even by Italians of the sixteenth century as highly as the creations of Raphael—if not above them.

In the same masterly way in which he carried out monumental works, Holbein occasionally designed decorations which served only to beautify some festivity which was quickly over. When Anne Boleyn rode in her coronation procession on the 31st May, 1533, from the Tower to Westminster, the streets by which the procession passed were richly and magnificently decorated. The most admired point on the whole route was the decoration planned by Holbein and erected by the merchants of the Steelyard. It was a stage with living pictures—such as the people of Antwerp had arranged on the occasion of the entry of Charles V.—and represented, on a magnificent Renaissance fabric, Parnassus with Apollo and the Muses.

The relations of Holbein with the Steelyard lasted several years. The dates on portraits of German merchants extend to 1536. From that time onwards his services were requisitioned by patrons of higher rank. By whose introduction he entered on relations with the Royal court, we do not know. For this period there is no information about his life except what his own works afford. His presentation at court cannot have been managed by Sir Thomas More, for the former Lord Chancellor was quite out of favour

Fig. 127. JANE SEYMOUR, QUEEN OF ENGLAND. Oil-painting in the Imperial Gallery, Vienna.
(After a photograph by J. Löwy, Vienna.)

on account of his decided disapproval of the steps by which King Henry VIII. brought about his breach with the Church of Rome; he ended his life on the scaffold on the 6th July, 1535, as a martyr to the constancy of his faith, jointly with Bishop Fisher, who was eighty years of age.

The first record of Holbein's intercourse with English gentlemen after his second arrival in London is to be found in the portrait of the royal falconer, Robert Cheseman, of the year 1533, in the Picture-gallery at the Hague. A man in his forty-eighth year, as stated on the picture, is represented at half-length, nearly the size of life, in a red silk doublet and black surcoat trimmed with fur; he carries the hawk — a splendid piece of painting — on his gloved left hand, and strokes it caressingly with his right hand; his face, with the sharp features and the eyes spying out some distant object, has itself assumed something of the character and expression of a falcon (Fig. 122). Of the year 1537 portraits are extant of persons who stood very near to King Henry VIII. This date is on a double portrait, in the collection of an English family, which bears the title of "The Ambassadors" and is renowned as one of Holbein's most important works, comparable, as regards execution, with the portrait of George Gisse. In one of the distinguished and learned gentlemen represented life-size and in whole length in this picture we can recognise the King's favourite, the "incomparable knight", Sir Thomas Wyatt.*) In a private collection in England there is a portrait of Thomas Cromwell which cannot have been painted later than the beginning of 1534; this date is fixed by a letter painted in the picture on which we can read the title of this man, who rose from a humble origin to an influential position and carried out the separation of the English from the Roman Church in a more far-reaching way than the King had originally intended.

In 1535 appeared a handsome edition of the whole of the Scriptures in the English language, translated by Coverdale. The book, which was not printed in England but at Zürich, was dedicated to Henry VIII. The title-page was adorned with a very fine border by Holbein. This design for the title is composed of a number of little pictures which contain corresponding pairs of events from the old and the new dispensation, according to mediaeval tradition, but treated in a new spirit. In the strip at the top the Fall and the Redemption are the subjects: at one side Adam and Eve under the tree, on the other the Saviour risen from the tomb, triumphant over Death and Hell. In both designs the figures are of surprising beauty. Then follow, down the sides, Moses receiving the Tables of the Law on Mount Sinai and Ezra reading the Old Law to the Jews on their return from the Babylonian Captivity, and, on the other side, Christ sending forth his disciples into all the world, and the Apostles preaching. At the bottom King David and the Apostle Paul stand facing one another. Between these two single figures we see Henry VIII. in kingly apparel sitting on the throne; before him kneel the Princes and Bishops of England and he bestows on the latter a book — the Holy Scriptures in the vulgar tongue. It is worth

---

*) Since this was written a document has come to light which proves that the two persons represented are Jean de Dinteville, French Ambassador to England in 1532—1533, and his friend Georges de Selve, Bishop of Lavaur, Ambassador to Charles V., who visited Dinteville in England. The picture has belonged since 1891 to the National Gallery. (Note by the translator.)

Fig. 128. HUBERT MORETT, GOLDSMITH TO KING HENRY VIII. Oil-painting in the Dresden Gallery.
(After an original photograph by Braun, Clément & Co., Dornach (Alsace) and Paris.)

observing that the King in this little picture — which, by the way, perhaps
through the wood-engraver's fault, is not a very good likeness — already wears
a beard, contrary to the habit prevailing up to that time in England, though,
thanks to his example, the fashion soon became universal.

At this period Holbein again made several designs on wood. In a few small cuts which were not published till after his death (in Archbishop Cranmer's Catechism) there is a reflection of the feeling excited by the frightful results of the official visitation of the English monasteries instituted by Cromwell. In these woodcuts, which represent the parable of the Pharisee and the Publican and Christ healing the man possessed of a devil, the Pharisees are drawn as monks. The latter small cut is signed by Holbein, contrary to his custom, with his full name. So, too, is a similar small woodcut which appeared in a pamphlet, a drawing of the Good Shepherd, in which the bad shepherd, who forsakes his flock, again appears as a monk. A series of small original drawings in the same spirit, but with still more pointed irony, the Passion of Christ, represented in twenty-two scenes, has disappeared. Sandrart, to whom they were shown by the Earl of Arundel, who then owned them, mentions them in his "Teutsche Akademie", and of sixteen of them there are engraved imitations of the seventeenth century, which convey merely an inacurate impression of the originals.

In 1535 Holbein drew a portrait on wood. The French poet, Nicolas Bourbon de Vandoeuvre, was then staying in England. Holbein painted his portrait and represented him in the act of writing; not, however, as in the case of the scholarly Erasmus, with downcast eyes, absorbed in what he was writing, but gazing into the distance with the pensive look of a poet. What the poet wrote during the sitting was a flattering expression of his admiration for the artist. From this portrait — the drawing for it is in the collection at Windsor Castle (Fig. 123) — Holbein afterwards made the likeness on wood, which was destined to adorn an edition of Bourbon's Latin poems. This edition appeared at Lyons in 1538, and in the same year Bourbon returned the painter's compliment in his own art: he was the author of the introductory verses in praise of Holbein's Old Testament cuts.

One of the aforesaid poems of Bourbon bears the heading; "On a picture by Hans, painter to His Britannic Majesty, and my friend". The picture which inspired the verses was the likeness of a sleeping boy, beautiful as a Cupid, painted on a tablet of ivory. It was, accordingly, a miniature. We have information, from other sources as well, that Holbein, who could paint with such extreme delicacy and carry out oil-paintings on quite a small scale with marvellous finish, made experiments in England in regular miniature-painting. Miniature-painting was at that time no longer exclusively what the original meaning of the word implies, the decoration of manu-scripts in colours, but the process used in painting books was applied to independent pictures on a very small scale. The word has ended by changing its meaning so completely that, nowadays, we describe any very small picture as a miniature, no matter in what technique it may be carried out.

Holbein is said to have learnt the process of miniature-painting by watching Lucas Horebout, a native of the Netherlands established at the

English court and brother of that
Susanna Horebout whose accomplishment in art Dürer had admired at
Antwerp and who was now living
in London as the wife of one of the
Royal archers. Holbein is said to
have far excelled his exemplar after
practising for a short time.

Many miniature-portraits in English collections, some of them painted
on pieces of playing-cards, pass for
works of Holbein. An undoubted
work of his hand is the little portrait,
dated 1535, of Henry Brandon, son
of the Duke of Suffolk, at the age
of five; it is in the library at Windsor
Castle (Fig. 114). Then there are
two portraits of 1536, forming a pair,
which belong to the Seymour family:
Henry VIII. and Jane Seymour, the
young queen who in May of this year
had succeeded the ill-fated Anne
Boleyn. In 1536 Holbein was court-
painter by appointment to Henry VIII.
and in receipt of a regular salary.
The first certain testimony to his
entering on this position is in a letter
which Nicolas Bourbon wrote from
home to a friend at the English
court: the poet sends his greeting
to several gentlemen at the court
and among them to "Master Hans,

Fig. 129. PRINCESS CHRISTINA OF DENMARK. Widowed
Duchess of Milan. Painting of 1538, belonging at the
Duke of Norfolk.

the Apelles of our time", and names him with the title "Royal painter",
as he does in the heading of the poem published two years later.

From this time onwards we find Holbein almost exclusively employed
as portrait-painter to the court of the King and to the highest aristocracy
of the land.

The highest rank among Holbein's portraits of the court belongs to
the likeness of Jane Seymour, now in the Imperial Gallery at Vienna (Fig. 127),
which is also the earliest in date.

The queen is represented at half-length, not quite life-size. She wears
a dark-red dress over a petticoat of silver brocade, matched by sleeves
of the same material. The pure, white complexion for which she was
famed comes out clear and cool against the purple tone of the dress on
the fair neck and the calm and modest-looking face surrounded by rich

Fig. 130. EDWARD, PRINCE OF WALES. Oil-painting in the Royal Picture-Gallery, Hanover.

ornaments in gold and jewels. The same fair skin appears in the delicate hands, which rest quietly one on the other in a way which admirably matches the expression of the face, and here it rivals the white of the cuffs of the sleeves, which are ornamented with costly work. It is a truly royal picture.

Henry VIII. had his portrait painted by Holbein in a wall-painting in the King's Chamber at Whitehall. The painting, which was finished in 1537, consisted of a combination of four full-length portrait figures on a rich, architectural background: Henry VIII., his parents, Henry VII. and Elizabeth of York, and his consort Jane Seymour; the two kings stand to the right in the picture (to the left, therefore, of the spectator), the queens to the left, the deceased sovereigns standing somewhat back and the

Fig. 131. ANNE OF CLEVES. Oil-painting on vellum, 1539. In the Louvre, Paris.
(After a photograph by Franz Hanfstängl, Munich.)

living couple in the foreground. Like all the monumental works of Holbein, this wall-painting has perished. It fell a victim to the fire at Whitehall in 1698. A small copy of it which King Charles II. had done is preserved in

the collection at Hampton Court. Still more important for the appreciation of this masterly work of Holbein is an extant portion of the cartoon which served to transfer the drawing of the picture to the wall. This portion, in the possession of the Duke of Devonshire, contains the figures of the two kings; it is not carried out, according to the usual style of such intermediate drawings, in charcoal, but with the brush, in black-and-white distemper. The print-cabinet at Munich possesses the study, drawn from life in the master's accustomed manner, for the head of Henry VIII. (Fig. 125). It it was the king's own idea to hand down to posterity the likeness of his person in a monumental painting and to let that whole painting consist merely of his own portrait, his wife's — whom he doubtless loved sincerely at the moment — and those of his parents, Holbein was certainly the very master to turn this piece of portraiture into a monumental picture of historical importance. In the figures of the deceased royal couple he put soul into the matter which extant portraits supplied to him. Of the living persons he has made magnificent studies of character, while copying them straight from life. Jane Seymour appears in the same character as in the oil-painting at Vienna, as the calm queen. Henry VIII. in most sumptuous apparel, bedecked with jewels, stands with his legs wide apart, stout and broadshouldered, with a head of a strong bony frame and soft flesh, with a hard and yet impressive look in his small eyes under their lofty arched eyebrows, and with a well-formed mouth of sensual and at the same time energetic expression, the whole face a picture of callousness, beneath which the more pleasing traits which nature had given it have disappeared; the right arm is placed akimbo with an air of defiance, while the left hand plays with the loop by which the dagger is suspended. Thus the King in the picture confronts the spectator as the Henry VIII. of history.

The extant oil-paintings which convey the likeness of the King are all reproductions of the fresco at Whitehall. Not one of them seems to be carried out by Holbein's own hand (Fig. 126).

According to all appearance, Henry VIII. was so completely satisfied with Holbein's presentment of him in the wall-painting at Whitehall that he considered it unnecessary to sit to him again for a later portrait.

A likeness of the King on wood — no sitting was required for that — was designed by Holbein as frontispiece to Hall's chronicle. In this large

Fig. 133. THOMAS HOWARD, DUKE OF NORFOLK. In the Royal Picture-Gallery, Windsor Castle.
(After an original photograph by Braun, Clément & Co., Dornach (Alsace) and Paris.)

woodcut Henry VIII. is represented on the throne, surrounded by his Councillors. The finest portrait by Holbein in any German collection must stand
very near, by its date, to the wall-painting at Whitehall. This is the portrait
of Hubert Morett in the Dresden Gallery (Fig. 128). This man did not
belong, it is true, to the great lords at court, but, for all that, he had a

great deal to do at the court. He was the King's jeweller. When he had
his life-size portrait taken by the court-painter it is evident that he declared
his wish to be taken in a similar attitude to that of his royal master. Like
him he is posed with his face exactly to the front, his right hand with the
glove off placed under the girdle and his left hand resting on his dagger.
It is interesting to compare this picture, in respect of the conception of
character which it displays, with the other masterpiece of Holbein's portrait-
painting which is to be found in Germany — the likeness of Gisse at Berlin.
The German merchant is represented engaged in his every-day business;
the English goldsmith stands before us in all his splendour. His stately
person and his rich costume fill the whole picture. A green silk curtain
forms the background, and creates, with the warm tone of the flesh and of
the reddish beard mingled with grey, with the gold ornaments, the black
satin, the brown fur and the white material of the inner garments such a
marvellous effect of colour as even Holbein himself never surpassed.

Morett may at that time have had frequent opportunities of coming
into close intercourse with Holbein, for he certainly must have carried out
many a handsome piece of work in gold and silver from the artist's designs.
The King made abundant use of his painter's accomplishment in designing
works of decorative art. Many drawings of Holbein for such objects are
preserved. Most of them are to be found in two sketch-books, one of
which is in the British Museum and the other in the Museum at Basle. In
the Basle book one of the drawings has the date 1537 by its side. These
are designs for all possible objects: vessels of various kinds, hand-mirrors
and other toilet-apparatus, handles for daggers, ear-rings, brooches and
other ornaments for gentlemen and ladies — every object a pattern of fine
taste in its general shape and in the rich decoration, almost always enlivened
by figures. A number of the drawings give merely figure-compositions
which were obviously intended as patterns for delicate ornamental work in
the precious metals. The subjects chosen are sometimes from mythology
or history of the classical period, sometimes from the Bible; religious and
allegorical motives, and heraldry also find a place. Mottoes, too, or other
inscriptions are frequently introduced, from which it can be inferred occasionally for what wearer the King, who probably in most cases gave the
order, intended the jewel. Holbein also exercised his power of artistic
invention on less important things than these, such as buttons, tassels,
braids and embroidery. Here, instead of his usual style, of giving relief and
picturesque effect, he adopted a style of arabesque ornament on the surface
in equally pure taste. One of his principal works is the design for a tall
cup with successive tiers of ornament, carried out with the pen with suggestions in colour of the combined effect of gold, pearls and precious stones.
The drawing is in the Bodleian Library at Oxford. The sumptuous vessel
was intended for the Queen, Jane Seymour; it bears her motto: "Bound
to obey and serve", and the joint initials H and I (Henry and Jane). None
of the most famous masters of ornamental art at the Renaissance surpasses

Fig. 134. PORTRAIT OF A MAN UNKNOWN, 1541. In the Royal Museum, Berlin.
(After a photograph by Franz Hanfstängl, Munich.)

Holbein in the richness and distinction of his taste. He reveals himself as a great master of ornamental style in architecture also in a drawing preserved in the British Museum containing the design for a chimney-piece, a structure in two storeys supported on columns, richly adorned with the most varied decorative designs and with figure-subjects. It can be re-

Fig. 135. CHARLES BRANDON, SON OF THE DUKE OF
SUFFOLK. Miniature-portrait, 1541. In the Library of
H. M. the Queen, Windsor Castle.
(After a photograph by Franz Hanfstängl, Munich.)

cognised by the introduction of the arms of England and the cipher of Henry VIII. as intended for a Royal palace.

In March 1538 Holbein travelled to Brussels on the business of the court. When Jane Seymour died soon after giving birth to a princess on the 12th October 1537, the King's Councillors, especially Thomas Cromwell, who now conducted the whole of the affairs of state, directed their thoughts to arranging a new marriage for the King as soon as possible. The King seemed at first to have no inclination for the project. But when, after various other continental princesses, the name of Christina of Denmark, the widow of Francesco Maria Sforza, Duke of Milan, was proposed, he took the matter seriously into consideration. The Princess, who had become a widow at the age of thirteen, was the daughter of King Christian II. of Denmark and Queen Isabella, the sister of the Emperor Charles V. Political reasons were in favour of a marriage with the niece of the Emperor, as a step towards more friendly relations with the latter and an inducement to him to forget the insult which Henry VIII. had put upon him by the repudiation of his first wife, Catherine of Aragon, aunt to Charles V. But, before all else, it was necessary to learn whether the princess gratified the King's personal taste. With that object Holbein was despatched to paint her portrait. On the 10th March 1538 he arrived, attended by a servant of Cromwell's, at Brussels, where the Duchess Christina was residing with her aunt, the Governess of the Netherlands. The English chargé d'affaires in Flanders, John Hutton, had meanwhile already sent off a portrait of the Duchess by a painter (whose name has not been recorded) for the King's benefit. However, when Holbein arrived, Hutton caused the messenger who was on his way with the picture to be stopped by an express courier, for he was of opinion, as he reported to Cromwell, that the portrait was "neither so good as the occasion required, nor as Master Hans would be able to do it". On the following day he craved permission of the Duchess to allow herself to be painted by the painter sent over for this purpose by the English court. On the very next day, the 12th march, the Duchess Christina gave Holbein a sitting. "Although he had only the space of three hours", so ran Hutton's report to Cromwell, "he showed himself a master of the art, for the likeness is quite perfect". The painting, which Holbein carried out from the sketch which he made in these three hours, probably a drawing in his well-known style, turned out a masterpiece. It is now the property of the Duke of Norfolk. Whereas the other painter

ANNO·DÑI·1541· ETATIS·SVÆ·28·

Fig. 136. PORTRAIT OF A MAN UNKNOWN, 1541. In the Imperial Gallery, Vienna.
(After a photograph by J. Löwy, Vienna.)

had portrayed the princess in great splendour of apparel, Holbein painted her just as she was at their first interview, in her Italian widow's dress. He painted her at full length, to show off her fine, tall figure. The girl of sixteen, still half a child, standing quite simply in the severe black dress, is a subject treated with truly great art, simple, natural, distinguished and sympathetic (Fig. 129).

In the summer of the same year the King sent the painter once more to the Continent, this time to Upper Burgundy — we do not know on what commission. On this occasion Holbein paid a short visit to his own people at Basle. He arrived there about the beginning of September. His fellow-citizens beheld with astonishment the painter, who had become so great a man abroad. "When he came back to Basle for a time from England, he was clad in silk and velvet, whereas before he had to buy wine at the tap". Such is the report preserved of him; in the eyes of his contemporaries it was a convincing sign of poverty when anyone had such wine as he needed fetched from the tavern, instead of keeping a supply in his own cellar. Holbein had every reason to congratulate himself on his position in England. In the account-books of the English court his salary since the spring of 1538 has been recorded: according to the proportionate value of money in those days it is calculated that his yearly pay amounted to the sum of £ 360 in modern currency. The government of Basle exerted itself once more, and that in good earnest, to secure the master for their own town. In a document of the 16th October 1538 the Burgomaster and Council promised "our dear citizen, Hans Holbein" a yearly salary of the quite respectable amount, for Basle in these days, of fifty florins, "for the special goodwill which we bear towards him because he is widely famed before all other painters for the abundance of his art; in consideration, further, that he may be serviceable to us with his advice in the affairs of our town, as regards building-operations and other matters whereof he has understanding, and that, finally, in case we have occasion to have some work of painting carried out, he may faithfully perform the same for us, always in return for a proper remuneration". Since it was to be expected, as Holbein declared, that he would hardly be able to depart from the English court with the King's consent within the next two years, leave was granted him for two years to return to England. During these two years, instead of the payment promised to him for his services, a yearly pension of forty florins was to be paid to his wife at Basle.

If on the expiration of his leave of absence for two years he should have settled again at Basle, he was to be in no way hindered, by drawing his salary from the town, from turning his art to account elsewhere. "Since we are well aware", so runs the remarkable passage relating to this point, "that the said Holbein cannot make the most profitable use of his art and work, which are far too valuable to be thrown away on old walls aud houses, in our service alone, we have, therefore, been pleased to grant a concession to the said Holbein that he may earn, take and receive fees for his art and handiwork from foreign kings, princes, lords and cities; that he may, further, convey and sell the works of art which he shall produce here among us to foreign lords in France, England, Milan and the Low Countries, once, twice, or thrice in the year, but each time with our special permission and not without our knowledge. Notwithstanding, he must not remain abroad deceitfully on the pretext of such journeys, but each time he shall bring his affairs speedily to a conclusion and thereupon betake himself home again without delay and place himself at our service, as stated above." Holbein accepted this offer and vowed and promised to observe the conditions attached to it. No doubt he was then firmly resolved to take up his permanent abode once more at Basle as soon as he should have earned a sufficient livelihood in England. He is said to have declared his intention of painting the frescoes in the town-

Fig. 137. SIMON GEORGE OF CORNWALL.
Oil-painting in the Städel Institute, Frankfurt am Main.
(After an original photograph by Braun, Clément & Co., Dornach (Alsace) and Paris.)

hall and other paintings over again, and in better style, at his own expense, since of his wall-paintings at Basle, only one, the house with the dance, struck him as "pretty good". But he never returned home.

In December 1538 Holbein was once more at the English court. A special bounty was paid to him for the King's business (not named) for the sake of which he had been despatched to the region of Upper Burgundy.

At the beginning of the next year he presented Henry VIII. with a portrait of little Prince Edward as a New Year's Gift; in return for this he received from the King "a gilt cruse with a cover". It is probable that Holbein could have done nothing to give his master greater pleasure; for Henry VIII., whose hopes of an heir to the throne had been so often frustrated, was quite in love with his little son, whom only specially favoured persons were permitted to approach. A life-size portrait in half length, now in the Picture-gallery at Hanover, may well be the picture just mentioned, to judge by the age of the child. The prince, aged two, shows his pretty little round face, over the brow of which falls a little fair hair, escaping from the front of the cap, and his fat little hands, relieved by a splendid costume of red and gold; he wears a frock of red velvet with gold lace

10*

and sleeves of cloth-of-gold, and over the child's cap a little red velvet bonnet with an ostrich-feather (Fig. 130). A charming little drawing in outline in the form of a medallion, showing the child at full length, sitting on a cushion and playing with a little dog, is among the drawings in the aforesaid sketch-book at Basle.

In July, 1539, Holbein was again sent off on his travels "on certain business" of the King's. The scheme of a marriage between Henry VIII. and the Emperor's niece had fallen through. He now, in defiance of the Emperor, contemplated an alliance with the daughter of a protestant German prince. Anne, sister of the Duke of Cleves and sister-in-law of the Elector of Saxony, was recommended to the King as a desirable match. Holbein travelled to Germany with a commission to paint her likeness. The King was so gallant as to send her his own portrait at the same time by the painter's hands; this information is derived from an entry in the account-books of the royal household, that Holbein was charged to take with him some object made by himself and paid for with a considerable fee, but not further named.

The likeness of the new royal bride was taken at the beginning of August at a castle in the Duchy of Cleves. On the 1st September the painter came back to London. If a fable gained currency at a later time, that Holbein painted the princess more beautiful than she really was and so induced the King to contract a marriage of which he soon repented, the portrait itself is preserved to prove the groundlessness of this assertion. The picture is in the Louvre. We see Anne of Cleves full-face in half-length, in stiff attire, with a quantity of jewellery, her pink and white face enclosed in a richly ornamented cap (Fig. 131). We see that Holbein found the lady uninteresting, and, in his honesty as an artist, he has presented her in the most uninteresting way. There is no movement in the figure, no movement in the features. How incomparably he has rendered the expression of the dull, German young lady, who "never left her mother's elbow!" In one point Holbein stands higher than all other great portrait-painters: in his grasp of character—even in the hands—in respect not only of form but also of expression. Just compare the folded hands of the three royal brides: Jane Seymour's in reserved repose, the Duchess Christina's expressive of good-nature and fidgetting like a child's, and those of the daughter of the Duke of Cleves, quite without animation! The ennui which the painter has felt is reflected even in the colour. As far as the subject goes, he had every means here of attaining a superb effect of colour; a fair skin, fine white material, red velvet, cloth-of-gold, gold and jewels —a splendour of colouring to which he gave suitable relief by a dark-green background. And yet with these means he has not produced any such charm of colour as he was generally able to evoke.

That Henry VIII. did not reproach his painter in respect of this portrait in the way which the historians relate, is proved by the manifestations of favour which were shown him immediately afterwards. In 1540 Holbein

Fig. 138. PORTRAIT OF A LADY UNKNOWN. In the Imperial Gallery, Vienna.
(After an original photograph by J. Löwy, Vienna.)

had his salary doubled. It is easy to understand how, under these circumstances, he resigned his intention of returning to Basle at the time agreed
upon. Holbein found an opportunity in London, too, of proving his skill
in building, on which the Council of Basle had counted especially. At least,
the richly ornamented ceiling of the Chapel in St. James's Palace, carried
out while Anne of Cleves was Queen, passes as a work of his design.

Fig. 139. SIR THOMAS WYATT. Drawing in black and coloured chalk.
Windsor Castle.
(After an original photograph by Braun, Clément & Co., Dornach (Alsace)
and Paris.)

Queen Anne was divorced.   Cromwell, the powerful and sagacious
conductor of English affairs of state, was beheaded.   The catholic Katherine
Howard became Queen and her uncle, Thomas Howard, Duke of Norfolk,
formerly a friend of Sir Thomas More and of the same way of thinking,
took the lead in public affairs; everything was changed once more at the
English court — but Holbein continued to enjoy the same favour.

Of Queen Katherine Howard no other portrait is known by Holbein's
hand but a miniature — like one which he had painted of Anne of Cleves
as a pendant to a similar portrait of the King; the little portrait is now in
the Library at Windsor Castle (Fig. 132).

A large and splendid portrait in the Picture-gallery of the same castle
introduces us to the Duke of Norfolk at the height of his power (Fig. 133).

Fig. 140. THE DUCHESS OF SUFFOLK. Drawing in black and coloured chalk.
Windsor Castle.

The Duke was sixty-six years of age when he was painted by Holbein.
He shows us a thin, reserved face, clean-shaven in the old-fashioned style;
over the wide turned-back lining of ermine with which his mantle is
trimmed, he wears the golden chain of the Order of the Garter; in his
delicate, lean hands he holds the white wand of the Lord Chamberlain and
the gold stick of the Earl-Marshal of England.

To the year 1541 belongs the miniature portrait of a boy of three, in
the Library at Windsor (Fig. 135). It represents Charles Brandon, second
son of the Duke of Suffolk, and forms a pendant to the likeness of his
brother Henry, painted six years earlier.

The date 1541 may be read on two portraits of gentlemen not belonging, apparently, to the circle of the court, one of which, a bust of a
man with a beard, treated with the most attractive simplicity (Fig. 134),
is in the Museum at Berlin, while the other, the half-length portrait of a

Fig. 141. Sir John Gage. Drawing in black and coloured chalk.
Windsor Castle.
(After an original photograph by Braun, Clément & Co., Dornach (Alsace)
and Paris.)

young man who sits behind a table with a book in his hand gazing at the spectator (Fig. 136), is in the Vienna Gallery.

Here we may mention two other master-pieces on a small scale in German collections, which belong to Holbein's English period, but furnish no means of fixing the date more exactly: the portrait of a good-looking young woman — a bust showing the hands — in the Vienna Gallery (Fig. 138), and the charmingly - conceived and exquisitely painted profile of a certain Simon George of Cornwall, in the Städel Institute at Frankfort (Fig. 137).

The portraits without any indication of the date are more numerous than those which are dated. It was an exceptional thing for Holbein to sign a picture with his name. He was sufficiently self-conscious to think, like Michelangelo, that his pictures conveyed in themselves the authentication of their origin. That is perhaps, what explains the fact why many a picture which has nothing in common with his art has at a later date been called by his name. How many portraits painted by Holbein in England are still extant has probably never yet been settled. They are, for the most part, scattered in private collections in England. Though there is nowhere any opportunity of seeing a considerable number of Holbein's painted portraits together, there is, on the contrary, a perfect treasure of his magnificent portrait-drawings collected in the library of Her Majesty the Queen at Windsor. This quite unique and priceless collection contains over eighty drawings — masterly throughout. In these first sketches from life, which sometimes tell all that is necessary in little more than outlines, sometimes are worked up to give the full effect of a painting, personages known and unknown, many of whom played their part in English history, meet the

Fig. 142. ELIZABETH, WIFE OF SIR HENRY PARKER. Drawing in black and coloured chalk. In the library at
Windsor Castle.
(After a photograph by Franz Hanfstängl, Munich.)

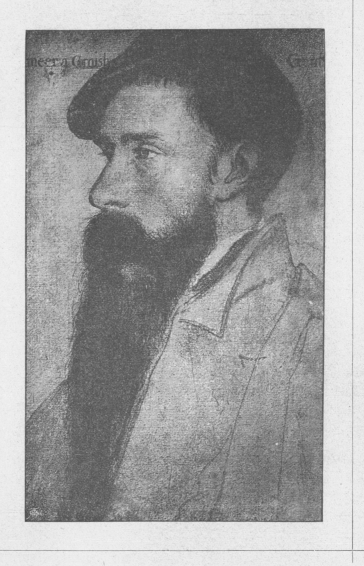

Fig. 143. RESKYMEER, A GENTLEMAN OF CORNWALL. Drawing in black and
coloured chalk. Windsor Castle.

eye with a vigour and a fulness of life almost equal to that of a finished
picture. In fact, there is quite a peculiar charm in these first records by
the artist's hand, which rapidly grasped the essentials and at the same time
made notes of everything which was to be expressed in the painting. That
so perfect a result is given with such slight means is the marvellous thing
in these drawings, which, without professing to be any thing finished in
themselves, are, for all that, complete works of art (Fig. 139—144).

In the same collection is a work by Holbein that is unique in its kind:
a composition of many figures carried out like a miniature; a drawing in

Fig. 144. LADY VAUX.
Drawing in black and coloured chalk. Windsor Castle.

silver-point, washed and charmingly enlivened with gold and a few tints. The subject represented is the visit of the Queen of Sheba to King Solomon. The mature beauty of the Renaissance architecture in this drawing should be observed, as it is very different to the architectural dreams of Holbein's youth (Fig. 145).

In 1542 there appeared a drawing by Holbein on the wood, which was, perhaps, the last work that he did by way of book-illustration. It is a portrait in medallion-form of Sir Thomas Wyatt and adorns the back of the title-page of a "Naenia" or elegy composed in memory of this favourite of the King, who died in 1541 in the flower of his age. Holbein has here drawn a speaking portrait with the greatest possible simplicity of line, which even the less practised hand of an English wood-engraver could follow.

In 1542 Holbein must again have painted a picture of the Prince of Wales. It is true that nothing is known of the picture itself, but among

Fig. 145. THE QUEEN OF SHEBA BEFORE SOLOMON. Washed drawing in the style of a miniature, enriched with gold and colours. In the library of H. M. the Queen, Windsor Castle.
(After an original photograph by Braun, Clément & Co., Dornach (Alsace) and Paris.)

the drawings at Windsor Castle there is one which shows the child at an age corresponding to this date (Fig. 141). The picture-gallery at the Hague possesses a work dated 1542, the excellent little portrait of a young man holding a falcon on his wrist. A portrait of Holbein by himself of this year is said to be extant in a private collection.

In the following year Holbein found leisure to paint himself twice, once

Edward Prince of Wales:

Fig. 146. EDWARD, PRINCE OF WALES. Drawing in black and coloured chalks in the library, Windsor Castle.
(After a photograph by Franz Hanfstängl, Munich.)

in miniature, the second time half the size of life. Both these portraits are lost. But of one of them two engravings of the seventeenth century convey an idea, one by Vorsterman (Fig. 148), the other by Wenzel Hollar, who also engraved many more of the works which Holbein did in England. The master, aged five-and-forty, has a very serious look. Following the

Fig. 147. John Chambers, physician to King Henry VIII. In the Imperial Gallery, Vienna.

universal costum he had let his beard grow, in imitation of the example set by King Henry. The portrait of Holbein by himself in the collection of portraits of painters in the Uffizi Palace, Florence is hardly any longer worthy of the name. It was, indeed, originally a portrait traced by Holbein apparently for the picture reproduced in the two engravings mentioned above; but the lines of the face have been disfigured by re-painting and have lost their resemblance.

At this time Holbein was working at a large picture containing many figures, which he was probably only able to finish by degrees. It was a portrait-group, which at the same time symbolised an historical incident.

Fig. 148. PORTRAIT OF HOLBEIN BY HYMSELF IN THE LAST YEAR OF HIS LIFE.
From Vorsterman's engraving after the lost original.

The united guild of the Barber-Sourgeons of London had it painted in commemoration of the grant of privileges to their society by the King. The representatives of the guild, eighteen in number, were depicted kneeling before the throne of Henry VIII., to receive from his hand their charter of liberties. Single persons among the members of the board were painted by Holbein separately, as well; for instance, Dr. John Chambers, one of the King's physicians, at the age of eighty-eight (Fig. 147). The fine picture of the dignified old man is now in the Imperial Gallery at Vienna. The large picture of the guild is also preserved; it still hangs in Barber's Hall, London. But it shows, apart from the injury which it has suffered by later re-paintings, that is was even originally only painted in part by Holbein. The master was not permitted to see this work finished.

In the midst of his productive activity Hans Holbein died, in the prime of life and far from home, in the autumn of 1543, probably as a victim to the plague, which was raging in that year at London.

His will is dated the 7th October. Not a word is said in it about his family at Basle. It is evident that he had provided for them beforehand; the family continued to live in easy circumstances after his death. His final testamentary dispositions only relate to the arrangement of his affairs in London. His horse and his other property were to be sold to discharge his debts to certain friends.

On the 29th November the goldsmith, John of Antwerp, one of the witnesses, renounced the execution of the will. Henry VIII. received a work from his artist's hand even after the latter's death. At the New Year of 1544 one of his chamberlains presented him with a sketch by Holbein for a tall clock, a large drawing in magnificent and tasteful style, which is now in the British Museum.